JAMES LASHER

THE
REVELATION
OF JESUS

CHARISMA
HOUSE

THE REVELATION OF JESUS by James Lasher
Published by Charisma House, an imprint of Charisma Media
1150 Greenwood Blvd., Lake Mary, Florida 32746

Copyright © 2025 by James Lasher. All rights reserved.

Unless otherwise noted, all Scripture quotations are taken from the New King James Version®. Copyright © 1982 by Thomas Nelson. Used by permission. All rights reserved.

Scripture quotations marked AMP are from the Amplified® Bible (AMP), Copyright © 2015 by The Lockman Foundation. Used by permission. www.Lockman.org

Scripture quotations marked ESV are from The ESV® Bible (The Holy Bible, English Standard Version®), copyright © 2001 by Crossway, a publishing ministry of Good News Publishers. Used by permission. All rights reserved.

Scripture quotations marked KJV are from the King James Version of the Bible.

Scripture quotations marked MEV are from the Modern English Version. Copyright © 2014, 2024 by Military Bible Association. Used by permission. All rights reserved.

Scripture quotations marked NASB are taken from the (NASB®) New American Standard Bible®, Copyright © 1960, 1971, 1977, 1995, 2020 by The Lockman Foundation. Used by permission. All rights reserved. www.lockman.org

While the author has made every effort to provide accurate, up-to-date source information at the time of publication, statistics and other data are constantly updated. Neither the publisher nor the author assumes any responsibility for errors or for changes that occur after publication. Further, the publisher and author do not have any control over and do not assume any responsibility for third-party websites or their content.

For more resources like this, visit MyCharismaShop.com.

Cataloging-in-Publication Data is on file with the Library of Congress.
International Standard Book Number: 978-1-63641-494-2
E-book ISBN: 978-1-63641-495-9

1 2025
Printed in the United States of America

Most Charisma Media products are available at special quantity discounts for bulk purchase for sales promotions, premiums, fund-raising, and educational needs. For details, call us at (407) 333-0600 or visit our website at charismamedia.com.

To all those who walk in obedience to the Lord, who surrender their own ways for His, even in the face of fear and uncertainty. To those who press forward, trusting in His call, knowing that true life is found only in obedience to Him.

Do you not know that to whom you present yourselves slaves to obey, you are that one's slaves whom you obey, whether of sin leading to death, or of obedience leading to righteousness?
—Romans 6:16

Obedience to God is the key to fulfilling the call He has placed on our lives. Without it, we will never realize the fullness of the life He has prepared for us.
To you, the faithful, this book is dedicated.

CONTENTS

	Introduction ix
Chapter 1	John's Greeting and Affirmation............ 1
Chapter 2	Loveless, Persecuted, Compromised, and Corrupted 19
Chapter 3	The Dead, the Faithful, and the Lukewarm...................... 36
Chapter 4	The Vision of the Throne................. 47
Chapter 5	The Lamb Unseals the Scrolls............. 56
Chapter 6	The Seals Broken 61
Chapter 7	The Sealed of Israel 71
Chapter 8	The Silence of Heaven.................... 75
Chapter 9	Demon Locusts and Angels............... 84
Chapter 10	The Mighty Angel 94
Chapter 11	The Two Witnesses 98
Chapter 12	John's Vision of the Woman 106
Chapter 13	The Beast from the Sea.................. 112

Chapter 14	The Lamb, the 144,000, and the Reaping 123
Chapter 15	The Lead-Up to the Bowl Judgments 130
Chapter 16	The Bowls of God's Judgment 138
Chapter 17	The Scarlet Harlot 158
Chapter 18	The World Mourns as Babylon Falls 164
Chapter 19	Heaven Rejoices 170
Chapter 20	The End of Time 178
Chapter 21	A New Heaven, Earth, and Jerusalem 186
Chapter 22	The Final Words of the Lord 193
	Conclusion 199
	A Personal Invitation to Know Jesus 203
	Notes 204
	Acknowledgments 212

INTRODUCTION

The Book of Revelation is perhaps the most vivid, mysterious book in the Bible.

There are multiple interpretations and theories about the events the Lord showed to His servant John. Some are almost universally accepted, while others are still the topic of discussion among theologians, philosophers, end-times experts, and everyday Christians.

This commentary is not intended to be a definitive, theory-establishing literary work.

On the contrary.

It is simply the take of a modern-day, average Christian who spends time daily in the Word, who has lived a life of sin but is redeemed by the grace of God, and who seeks to ignite discussion about what I find to be the most captivating book in Scripture.

But perhaps most of all my hope for anyone who reads this book is that they turn toward the Scriptures, read the Book of Revelation for themselves, and just see what the Lord puts on their heart while digging into the Word of God.

This is not to say any other books are lesser than Revelation. Not even in the slightest. This is merely a look into the most definitive work on the end-times that God provided to us. There are, of course, other books that discuss this topic: the Prophets, 2 Thessalonians, Jesus' own words in Matthew 24, and much more. Perhaps I will eventually write commentaries on those, but in the meantime I am doing this only because I feel the Lord has put it on my heart to do so.

It's as simple as that.

As someone who works in the media, I see more of what's happening in the world than the average person, through the lens of both secular and Christian media outlets. Allow me to be frank: The state of the world is not good.

The hope of Jesus is still alive and well in the world, but evil is taking large swaths of ground in the spiritual battle taking place around us. I wholeheartedly believe we are in the days leading up to the great tribulation.

I do not believe we are there yet; however, we are well on our way.

This book is meant to compare the events of today to what the Book of Revelation discusses—what have we seen so far, what has been fulfilled, what hasn't?

To be sure, Satan is making moves in the world today that he was previously unable to make. I believe this is because the Lord is allowing him to achieve the goals that will lead to his ultimate confrontation with Jesus Christ, the King of kings and Lord of lords.

For Satan to reach this endgame between him and the risen Lord, things must get worse in the world, and we are seeing this on a daily basis.

God's design is under attack in every way. Gender, sexuality, governance, the family, the church, faith, politics, and the list goes on—all are under immense spiritual warfare.

But God gave His followers a tool, a hope, that is invaluable: His holy Word, the Bible.

Looking at the events taking place today will open your eyes to the true agenda behind what is unfolding: a worldwide, global digital currency; a one-world government; attacks on Christians and Jews; efforts to silence pro-God and pro-freedom speech; and control over all aspects of human life. All these things and more make complete sense when put in the proper context: the God context.

So that is what I hope you will take away from reading this: a modern perspective on the events shaping the eventual return of Jesus Christ and the establishment of His everlasting kingdom.

In this hope, I believe I speak for many when I say, "Come, Lord Jesus."

CHAPTER 1

JOHN'S GREETING and AFFIRMATION

It is amazing how, right out of the gate, John establishes not just the source and authenticity of the Book of the Revelation of Jesus Christ, or Revelation, as we simply call it, but also the authority with which the Revelation was given.

> The Revelation of Jesus Christ, which God gave Him to show His servants—things which must shortly take place. And He sent and signified it by His angel to His servant John, who bore witness to the word of God, and to the testimony of Jesus Christ, to all things that he saw.
> —Revelation 1:1–2

The Revelation flowed from God the Father to Jesus Christ the Son, who is the Word of God, to His angel until finally reaching the initial human destination—John, the beloved disciple and one of the "Sons of Thunder" (Mark 3:17).

This "chain of command," as we call it in the military, is such a strong reflection of the orderliness of God. Whenever we see chaos, confusion, or disorder in society, this is not from God. There are certainly times when we may not understand what God is doing in our lives, but as John begins the book, we see God doing things in an orderly, nonchaotic fashion.

Interestingly, John continues in verse 2 by establishing the authority granted to him by the Lord Most High. Much as Paul does throughout his letters, John lays claim to this authority as a disciple of Jesus Christ who personally witnessed the death and resurrection of Jesus.

The Revelation of Jesus

John was chosen and justified as the Lord's recipient of the Revelation.

God is above human reasoning to be sure, but when you look at John, it makes sense (to me at least) why he was chosen to receive the Revelation.

I would argue that few had the authority John had in the spiritual realm. Yes, Peter was so anointed that the Holy Spirit used his shadow to heal. Paul evangelized much of the known world at the time, but John is different.

Jesus loved all His disciples, including Judas, who He knew would eventually betray Him. But John was uniquely spared the fate met by many of the other original Twelve, including John's own brother, James, whom Herod put to death (Acts 12:1-3).

- Judas Iscariot, the infamous betrayer, was overcome with guilt after handing Jesus over to the authorities for thirty pieces of silver and took his own life by hanging himself.
- James (son of Zebedee), one of Jesus' closest disciples, was the first apostle martyred when he was executed by King Herod Agrippa I, likely by the sword.
- Peter—bold, fiery, and always at the forefront—was eventually crucified upside down in Rome under Emperor Nero. Tradition says this was at his own request because Peter believed himself unworthy to die in the same manner as Christ.
- Andrew, Peter's brother and the one who brought him to Jesus, was crucified in Greece on an X-shaped cross, a symbol still associated with him today.

- Philip is believed to have been martyred in Hierapolis (modern-day Turkey), though accounts vary.
- Bartholomew, often identified as Nathanael, is believed to have met one of the most brutal fates—being flayed alive, meaning he was skinned.
- Thomas, who famously doubted Jesus' resurrection until he saw His wounds for himself, is believed to have taken the gospel to India, where he was impaled for his faith.
- Matthew, the former tax collector, was likely martyred, possibly in Ethiopia, though details are unclear.
- John, the only apostle who wasn't martyred, spent his final years in Ephesus and died of natural causes, though he endured exile on the island of Patmos beforehand.
- James (son of Alphaeus) is believed to have been stoned.
- Simon the Zealot is an apostle who, according to tradition, was martyred in a gruesome way—by being sawed in half.
- Thaddeus (also known as Jude) is by some accounts said to have been martyred by being beaten.[1]

As you can see, all but John was martyred.

Jesus loved John so much that it is discussed in the Word of God, and he was called *beloved* by the Messiah. John was the one entrusted with the most secret of prophecies given by the Lord through His messengers.

The Father gave the Revelation, and the Son chose the vessel who would receive it.

What an honor.

This special relationship was built during Christ's time on earth, and the devotion John had for Jesus carried on after His ascension. A bond like this reminds me of David and Jonathan's—it is a brotherly love yet is also submissive, as both John and Jonathan recognized the person the Lord had anointed king. Having such a strong bond with Jesus, I imagine John felt much emotional pain at the departure of his Lord—a hurt deeper than David's pain after the death of Jonathan. The world tries to twist such bonds between friends to fit its corrupt version of the Bible, but there was no carnality in these relationships.

John also was the one who was with Jesus in the Garden of Gethsemane, at the cross, at His resurrection, and at His ascension, and he was present at Pentecost. He seems like the perfect candidate to receive this most important prophecy.

The person who received the words of the Father, the only One who knows the time of the Son's return, had to be the most trusted among all Jesus' followers. Just as Moses was able to confidently and humbly say he was the humblest man in the world (Num. 12:3), so too could John claim the title of the most trusted—for unto him was given the Revelation.

As many before me have already said, John informs us we will be blessed by simply reading the Book of Revelation: "Blessed is he who reads and those who hear the words of this prophecy, and keep those things which are written in it; for the time is near" (1:3). That alone should set off alarms in our spirits about just how important it is to read and study this book (while not ignoring the other books of the Bible, of course). It is the key to understanding the events that are to take place before the literal end of the world. As John writes, "the time is near."

Verse 3 also denotes the urgency for John to tell the message, not for a specific point-in-time emergency but for those who heed the Word to come to obedience and spread the gospel so the eventual calamity will not claim as many souls as Satan would like.

I find it quite interesting, and hope you do too, that in Revelation 1:4–8 John takes on what feels like a Pauline introduction to the seven churches in the Roman province of Asia (Asia Minor, or modern-day Turkey).[2] John greets the churches with warmth but also, again, stands firm in his apostolic authority as one of the Twelve.

Do we respect authority like that today? I do not believe we do, simply because the society we live in, and even the church, is filled with so much disrespect.

Have you seen or heard people question their pastors or ministry leaders because they did not understand what their pastors were doing, instead of placing faith in both their leadership and the God who positioned them there? If your answer is, "Well, so many have fallen from grace in leadership," that is not a sufficient excuse to disrespect the authority the Bible says God put in place (Rom. 13:1).

Of course, this is not to say that asking a pastor for clarification or having questions about something is a sin—certainly not. But where is your heart? John's was in a place of love for the churches he was writing to—past, present, and future. He wrote to them in obedience, hoping to ignite true repentance, rekindle their passion for God, and realign them with His righteousness.

THREE IN ONE

In this introduction to the seven churches, John continues the amazing theme that I believe is the high point of the Bible, which encompasses everything else: the lordship of Jesus Christ.

Again, within the first five verses of Revelation we see

another factor of three in place. John describes Jesus as "the faithful witness, the firstborn from the dead, and the ruler over the kings of the earth" (1:5).

Here is one way I view verse 5, which has several different interpretations, all which are as valid as what I am presenting. Jesus was God's witness in all things. He was there at the beginning. He witnessed the evil of man and the grace and mercy of God, who offered them reprieve time and time again.

Jesus witnessed God's plan of salvation unfold after He nearly wiped out humanity with a flood. He witnessed the establishment of the Abrahamic and Mosaic covenants. He witnessed it all and, in His sinless perfection, pleaded mankind's case before the Lord in the courts of heaven when He overcame sin and death. He is our bridge to salvation before the Father.

Jesus is "the firstborn from the dead." There are always examples of those who were raised from the dead by the power of God, yet they all eventually succumbed to death. Taking Enoch and Elijah out of the equation—as they have not yet tasted death, and many predict they are the two witnesses we will see later in the book—Jesus tasted death and then overcame it! Here is where His life is different than those of the boy Elisha raised from the dead and of Jesus' friend Lazarus: Jesus never died again after the resurrection, and He never will. He overcame death and will never be subject to it again. He holds power over it.

One thing I have learned in my walk with the Lord is that when Jesus witnessed death, He did so in a manner none of us can even imagine, having taken all humanity's sin upon Himself. It was a spiritual, mental, and emotional weight so great (added to the physical weight and pain of being crucified) only the Father could comprehend the magnitude of the sacrifice required to absolve His creation, mankind, of sin. So great was this burden—and I feel we often overlook this aspect—that Jesus asked the Father to remove that cup from Him. Yet still in the face of this great undertaking, He submitted Himself to the Father's will, for Jesus was the only One capable of making this sacrifice as the spotless Lamb.

Looking at notes about John's wording in describing Jesus in verse 5, we see he uses the term *martus* (*martys*), or *martyr*, which is translated "witness" in the New King James Version.[3]

How fitting is this? While Stephen was the first recorded follower of Jesus who was martyred for his faith in the Messiah, Jesus was the first (and ultimate) martyr. Jesus was killed for telling the truth—that He is the way, the truth, and the life, and no one will go before the Father except through Him (John 14:6). This is the same message proclaimed by Stephen, James, Peter, and every believer who has lost their life following the footsteps of their Savior, Jesus Christ.

Jesus being described as a witness, or martyr, first highlights His divine servanthood and submission to the will of the Father, setting the example for all His followers to emulate. But Jesus' acts of servitude were many, like washing the disciples' feet. He demonstrated this amazing level of humility throughout His life, putting the will of God before His own in all things, even unto death.

John then praises Jesus for the love He showed to all by the shedding of His blood (Rev. 1:5). It is this blood, this precious blood, that John explains washed away the sins of mankind, and in that blood flows the power of Jesus' victory over death. This victory, along with the authority bestowed upon the Son, granted Him the right to make His followers kings and priests, not only in the present day but also in eternity, where they will rule and reign with Him forever.

It is this designation as kings and priests in verse 6 that marks the authority given to us. Being empowered spiritually by the Holy Spirit, Christians have the power and authority to cast out and command demonic spirits, just as the apostles demonstrated in the Bible.

This designation also brings with it immense responsibility, for we are Jesus' representatives on earth. His commands and the Word of God must be obeyed, for as history has shown, a church not led in Christlike love, obedience, and Holy Spirit power can have disastrous results. Even worse, it will tarnish the perfect name of Jesus.

After giving Jesus a worthy introduction, we see John sort of kick things up a notch in verse 7, if you catch my meaning.

> Behold, He is coming with clouds, and every eye will see Him, even they who pierced Him. And all the tribes of the earth will mourn because of Him. Even so, amen.
> —Revelation 1:7

Now suddenly we are getting a quick glimpse into Jesus' triumphant return as the warrior King. His return is not reminiscent of the baby born in a manger, when the heavens were filled with angels praising the amazing moment. No, Jesus is coming, and He is coming with a mission, with authority.

When Jesus returns, He is coming in a physical form, flanked by clouds of God's presence, reminiscent of how the Israelites were guided by the presence of God through the wilderness of Sinai (Exod. 13:21).

This great event will be viewed by all, whether simultaneously through a move of God in the supernatural, by way of modern-day media, or as He encircles the earth. None will deny the return of the King.

This transition in verse 7—going from the servant leadership of Jesus to His authority, which is given to Him by the Father, as the King over all the earth and its inhabitants—highlights the stark difference in how Jesus is viewed and portrayed in the Gospels versus what the following chapters in Revelation will describe.

Is it not amazing how God orchestrated the Bible to authenticate itself?

What an event the return of Jesus is going to be when He makes His presence known to all the world in glorious victory. The earth will recognize not only its one true King but also its judge.

Some people may be a little more distraught at that realization than others. All who are of the world will weep bitterly, yet those of the tribe of the Lion of Jesus—Jesus Christ—will end up rejoicing because they will never again have a cause for mourning.

Jesus' subsequent declaration in verse 8 as the Alpha and the Omega (the First and the Last) signifies His divinity over all things: time, places, and people.

> "I am the Alpha and the Omega, the Beginning and the End," says the Lord, "who is and who was and who is to come, the Almighty."
> —REVELATION 1:8

He was the Word during creation and before time began. He encompasses everything as the First and the Last and therefore has authority and power over all that is created.

His declaration is one of power. You can read it and feel it jumping off the pages of the Bible. It is such an authoritative statement that Jesus declares it and has John write it twice in the first chapter of the Revelation (vv. 8, 11)!

The resurrected King's power and authority are recognized in all places, even a place beyond time and space. Because eternity is a place, event, and time to come, Jesus establishes His authority over that as well.

This return, this amazing event that will alter the course of humanity unlike anything ever seen before, is the finalizing of His victory at the cross.

Another interesting fact that stuck out to me in verse 8 is John's reference to the Lord as the One "who is and who was and who is to come." This threefold description has three more insights held within it:

1. It speaks of God the Father, God the Son, and God the Holy Spirit.

2. It points to the fact that each of those roles is revealed in the Son: He was the Word at the beginning; He came and (three more!) lived on earth, died for the sins of mankind, and rose again, defeating sin and death; and He has yet to return to collect His bride and defeat Satan once and for all.

3. It represents the three distinguishable eras from the establishment of God's Law: the Mosaic era, when the Jews lived by the Law; the period after Jesus fulfilled the Law and bridged the gap for everyone to find salvation and be reconciled with the Father; and the time yet to come after Christ has established His reign forever.

How amazing is God? Three messages in three descriptions from the God who is three in one.

As we arrive slowly but surely at verse 9, John, in similar fashion yet again to Paul (are you noticing a trend here?), explains he too is a partaker in the suffering of Christ.

John had lived through the death of his brother and had most likely heard of, if not witnessed, the deaths of many other early Christians.

As strong in the Lord as John was, this must have weighed heavily on him. He was still human after all. But through it all

John's Greeting and Affirmation

he remained faithful, proving again that the Lord had chosen the right vessel to receive the Revelation.

John emphasizes his apostolic authority by identifying with the suffering that comes from being faithful to Jesus. He's speaking not just as an observer but as a fellow believer who has endured persecution for his faith. However, he also points to the greater reality that suffering for Christ is not the end—it is tied to both the kingdom and the future glory that believers will share with Christ. In this John reminds his readers that hardship is a part of the Christian life, but it also comes with the promise of ruling and reigning with Christ in His kingdom. This helps encourage us as we read his words that the ending is worth the journey. We will always encounter storms in our lives, but as John encourages, we will also partake in the glory of Jesus Christ.

Being a believer often brings with it a misrepresentation of what the Christian life truly entails. All too often we are told of only one side of the story.

Yes, we are forgiven and saved by a God who loves us (John 3:16), and there are blessings that come with being faithful servants of Jesus Christ. But there are also sufferings, tears, and heartache.

Paul writes in 2 Corinthians 1:8, "For we do not want you to be ignorant, brethren, of our trouble which came to us in Asia: that we were burdened beyond measure, above strength, so that we despaired even of life."

This is not meant to be a downer or make it seem like the Christian walk is wretched and bleak. Not at all. It is merely meant to paint the full picture of life before the establishment of God's perfect kingdom: There is joy and sadness, laughter and tears, love and heartache. We are still in a world cursed with sin, and until sin is done away with for good, pain will continue.

It is when we are filled with the Holy Spirit, however, that we display the fruit of the Spirit and are given the supernatural strength to endure, persevere, thrive, grow, and learn through trying times.

As part of John's justification for writing as a sufferer and companion in the "tribulation and kingdom and patience of Jesus Christ" (Rev. 1:9), he explains exactly where he was when the Revelation was given.

Patmos is an island in the Aegean Sea and was used as a penal colony during the time John was exiled there.[4] Those without the Holy Spirit, which John had, must have been hopeless and in despair on the island. John, however, could endure with patience and peace, for his current situation could not imprison his soul, as the Revelation would prove.

I hesitate to say John was imprisoned while on Patmos, as his spirit remained free in Jesus Christ. John clearly maintained his spiritual strength and maturity.

How often do we allow our situations to dictate our spiritual conditions? I certainly am guilty of it, but John was on that next level of maturity. He was able to discern the voice of the risen Lord because he spent his time "in the Spirit" (v. 10). All Christians today would greatly benefit from spending more time engaging in this practice.

> I was in the Spirit on the Lord's Day, and I heard behind me a loud voice, as of a trumpet.
> —REVELATION 1:10

Spending this time in the Spirit implies John regularly utilized his "prayer language," as many tend to call it. John wrote that he was "in the Spirit" as though it was a common occurrence, something he practiced regularly. The presence of the Holy Spirit is a place of peace, healing, and restoration—things John was probably in great need of, considering his situation and the persecution facing the church.

Like Paul's Damascus-road encounter with Jesus Christ

when Paul experienced the flash of light that only he saw (Acts 9:3), or like when Balaam's donkey saw the Angel of the Lord (Num. 22:23), John was the only one to hear the trumpet sound in the Spirit behind him. It is possible that he was alone, but being on a penal colony island, there is a good chance that others may have at least been around him at the time, but this is mere speculation on my part.

But this message was for John (at the time), and John alone. He was entrusted with the Revelation, and he alone on all the earth would see what took place in the Spirit. It was his charge to disseminate this heavenly message for the rest of the world to hear of and prepare for.

THE ALPHA AND OMEGA

With this supernatural trumpet blast, in verse 11 John was again addressed by his one true love, the Messiah, who said, "I am the Alpha and the Omega, the First and the Last," and, "What you see, write in a book and send it to the seven churches which are in Asia: to Ephesus, to Smyrna, to Pergamos, to Thyatira, to Sardis, to Philadelphia, and to Laodicea." To be spoken to directly by his old friend who was greater than a friend, his teacher, would surely cause a physical reaction in John from the Spirit, much like travailing in prayer does.

This is now the second time in the first chapter alone that Jesus has proclaimed His divinity and authority over all that is or was, calling Himself "the Alpha and the Omega, the First and the Last."

The Trinity's power and scope are detailed in this proclamation. Jesus previously stated all that He has, is, and does is from the Father, yet Jesus has authority over all things.

Jesus sent the Holy Spirit as the helper to His followers until He returns as the triumphant and victorious King of kings and Lord of lords.

Each member of the Trinity is a part of the others and is outside human comprehension. Each yields to the others, yet each has full authority over all, for each is fully God.

Three in One, One in Three.

As Jesus spoke to John, the message He had was for seven specific churches in the region of Asia, but the message is alive and well for the church today as well!

There was a moment, as the text says in verse 12, when John turned and recognized the voice of the ascended Lord. Perhaps wonder and expectation shot through him at the possibility of seeing Jesus in all His glory again, but this time it was the transformed King Jesus.

How long had John wondered if he would see Jesus again? Many of his fellow Christians had already been killed physically before Jesus returned. As a human, John must have had moments of questioning. Then, he got a reveal to rival all reveals:

> I saw…in the midst of the seven lampstands One like the Son of Man, clothed with a garment down to the feet and girded about the chest with a golden band. His head and hair were white like wool, as white as snow, and His eyes like a flame of fire; His feet were like fine brass, as if refined in a furnace, and His voice as the sound of many waters; He had in His right hand seven stars, out of His mouth went a sharp two-edged sword, and His countenance was like the sun shining in its strength.
> —REVELATION 1:12–16

This must have been such a moment of confirmation of all the things John had held on to and believed, even during the trying times he had endured leading to this moment.

I have been nothing but blessed by my *New Spirit-Filled Life Bible*, put together under the executive leadership of the dearly departed Pastor Jack Hayford, and in Revelation the classical notes section is written by Earl W. Morey, PhD, while the dispensational interpretation is written by Coleman Phillips, DDiv. Within the notes, it gives a listing of the meanings behind the descriptions of Jesus' appearance in verses 13–16, which I would like to share with you:

> The clothing of the Lord symbolizes priestly royalty; the **white hair** and flaming **eyes** symbolize eternity, wisdom, and omniscience; the **fine brass** [describing His feet] suggests immutability and omnipotence; the **many waters** [His voice] represent commanding authority.[5]

Everything involving Jesus has a purpose. That is why those who use biblical discernment in today's world can recognize what is of God and what is not. Allow me to explain.

God is *the* God of purpose and order. He created order out of chaos during creation, and one of the many tests I apply to events, movements, ideologies, and leaders in the world is this: Are they people of purpose and order?

Now, this is not the only test to determine if someone is righteous according to the principles of God written in the Bible, but it is a great start and has aided me in learning and growing in biblical discernment.

Chaos and distortion are not the ways of God. When a movement is steeped in lawlessness and disorder, such as the counterculture revolution the United States experienced beginning in the 1960s, it is safe to say these actions do not align with the will or design of God. Instead, they are the ways of the world.

Also, because people like to argue so much about what color Jesus' skin was, let us note that Scripture tells us right here: brass. Case closed.

Awesome does not quite describe the vision of Jesus before John. Giving credit where it is due, John is able to transcribe what can only be called the most intense vision anyone in the history of humanity has been given. That takes some incredible presence of mind after witnessing all that John sees.

Symbolically, verses 13-16 are rich with information. As previously mentioned, everything about Jesus' clothing and appearance has meaning, as well as the seven lampstands representing the seven churches Jesus is addressing in the letters John is writing. I am of the belief that the seven stars represent the angels set forward as guardians over the churches (as Jesus later addresses in the chapter). Also meaningful are the two-edged sword (my personal favorite), which is the Word of God, and His countenance like that of a sun. Jesus' might and glory are so powerful He is like a walking supernova, but even more powerful than an exploding sun.

And what does John do after taking all this glory in? He just falls out in verse 17 as though he were dead! But who can blame him? Who has ever seen Jesus in such glory and might?

John is a witness to such a monumental moment, and how does Jesus respond? By comforting His old disciple and friend, assuring him he has nothing to be afraid of (v. 17).

Can you imagine? In all Jesus' glory John still recognizes his Savior. He also recognizes the power and authority that literally radiate from Jesus. John understands the magnitude of seeing Jesus as no other human has ever seen Him, not even Paul—for Paul saw Christ in His full glory not in the Spirit but with his eyes, even though the others did not (Acts 9:3–9).

Just as Balaam had his eyes opened to what his donkey saw (Num. 22:31), Paul's eyes were opened to see Jesus. This is why Paul's eyes needed healing afterward, yet John's do not (from what we read)—because John sees what physical eyes could not see at the time, the full might of Jesus, and he rightly prostrates himself before the conqueror of death.

Jesus recognizes this, not that we're getting anything past Him anyway, but He accepts John's submission before Him.

He knows John loves Him. He even acknowledges their past relationship by laying His glory-filled hand on John's shoulder in reassurance to His disciple of old (Rev. 1:17).

The relationship has evolved, however, and matured, as John himself has as well. There is still the closeness that was once there, along with a severity that John recognizes. He is looking at the King of kings and Lord of lords. Sin cannot be tolerated in His presence and will be eradicated by His hands. Yet despite this Jesus loves John for his faithfulness, endurance, suffering, loyalty, and righteousness. I personally believe John was the closest and most loving of all the disciples.

While Jesus reassures John, as a loving Lord and Savior would do, He reaffirms and declares His power and authority over all things, places, people, and time for the third time in the first chapter of Revelation.

> I am He who lives, and was dead, and behold, I am alive forevermore. Amen. And I have the keys of Hades and of Death.
> —REVELATION 1:18

This repetition of His position in the grand scheme of reality and all that was, is, and will come shows us just how important Jesus' place, authority, and names truly are.

After this brief moment between the two, Jesus does not waste time in getting across His message, justifying Himself and His identity before John.

The earthly Jesus that John knew, who lived, died, rose again, and ascended before John's very eyes, is alive forevermore because of His victory over death. This victory granted Him the authority to hold the keys to hades and death.

Now Jesus holds control over death, as do those who believe in Him, which is why Paul encourages fellow believers to rejoice in His victory over death (1 Cor. 15:55–57)!

We are going to reign with Jesus, free from the grip of death. What a time that is going to be. The imagination does not even begin to do it justice.

Having established His identity, authority, and kingship, in the final two verses of chapter 1 Jesus commands John to write down all that he sees—the Revelation. This book that will bless the reader was meant from the beginning to be read and meditated on.

The events John would write down would have an immediate effect but would also be repeated throughout history, and they will continue in relevance and truth until the end-times and the establishment of Jesus' eternal kingdom.

Jesus ends the first chapter of Revelation with an explanation of what John sees in His hands—one of many explanations He gives throughout the book.

> The mystery of the seven stars which you saw in My right hand, and the seven golden lampstands: The seven stars are the angels of the seven churches, and the seven lampstands which you saw are the seven churches.
> —REVELATION 1:20

This is the foundation of the letters John writes to the seven churches because now he understands the who, what, and where of the words he is writing. Each letter in turn builds upon this knowledge, revealed by Jesus Christ.

CHAPTER 2

LOVELESS, PERSECUTED, COMPROMISED, and CORRUPTED

How could a church that proclaims the name of Jesus Christ get to such a state that it is considered loveless? Jesus' entire life and ministry were rooted in love for God's creation—humanity.

John 3:16 explains this perfectly.

Not only that, but these were the two commandments Jesus gave His disciples and the Pharisees: to love the Lord your God with all your heart and to love your neighbor as yourself (Matt. 22:36–40). Love is also the very first fruit of the Spirit listed in the Bible!

In case you have not caught on yet, love is exceedingly important to God.

That is why Satan attacks love with bitterness, resentment, and hatred at every opportunity. Humanity's love can grow cold, hearts can harden, and tempers can flare in the absence of the Holy Spirit in people's hearts.

This loveless attitude has plagued the church for centuries, as numerous times, those who claim to be followers of Christ have not loved their fellow man or, even more importantly, have not loved the Lord their God.

I believe this is why in Revelation 2 Jesus commands John to write to the angel, or spirit, guiding and protecting the church at Ephesus, the loveless church, first.

Because they had forgotten their first love.

EPHESUS: THE LOVELESS CHURCH

Much like the angel in the Book of Daniel, this angel needed prayer and assistance for its battles against the enemy. This would help ensure that spiritual strongholds would not take shape and form within the church it was charged with overseeing.

Jesus reassures both the angel and the church with a reminder of His authority and power. He explains to John that He holds the spirits of the churches in His hand and can walk unimpeded between the churches as He wills.

With how often Jesus has discussed His power and authority, Christians really need to take seriously the fear of the Lord we are supposed to demonstrate by how we live our lives. This is a trait many have forgotten, as they live lackadaisical, lukewarm lives. But we'll get to that later.

One aspect of this letter, for me, is often mistaken. I have categorized these letters as something John has written to the churches. But that would be incorrect.

These letters are from Jesus to His churches. While John did indeed transcribe them—he did the grunt work, as we say—Jesus wrote these letters and spoke them to John to take down.

When He begins the letter to the first church, Ephesus, the resurrected Lord builds up the angel of the church. He certainly is our Comforter and, as David said many times, our place of peace. Jesus encourages the church and acknowledges all the good that has been at the church with the spiritual overwatch of their angel.

Have you ever been in ministry and, during a low moment, wondered if God even knew what you were doing? I know I have at times, and I can assure you God sees everything we do in service to Him.

In the spirit of these moments Jesus highlights the constant struggle for those who bear His name. And it really is a constant battle, or "race," as Paul describes it (1 Cor. 9:24). The devil is always looking for a crack, an opening, to get his foot in the door and derail our relationship with and kingdom building for the Lord.

The church at Ephesus had fallen into a trap many have fallen into long after the physical church of Ephesus was gone: the trap of religion and of a religious spirit, an unbending and merciless spirit that casts judgment and carries itself in a haughty fashion. Now the church at Ephesus found itself, as do those afflicted with a religious spirit, removed from the relational love of Christ that empowers the church (His bride) to spread the gospel with great effect.

As much love and care as Jesus shows His beloved church, He cannot abide or tolerate this lapse of Christlike love, for as previously mentioned, it is one of the commandments given to His disciples before His ascension. Paul reinforces this commandment in 1 Corinthians 13, identifying love as the greatest gift and as mandatory for the Christian walk.

Easier said than done, huh?

The world we live in today has a severe shortage of Christlike love within it. This is not to say it is not there, but societies and cultures around the world have been infected with hard hearts that do not love their neighbors. Tribalism is the name of the game now, and if you are not for someone, you are against them.

Abiding by His long-suffering nature, Jesus still gives this type of church a chance to repent before judgment is carried out—a chance to return to how things were when the love of Christ burned within their hearts.

This forsaking of Christ's commandment and, in turn, of Him brings with it a grave punishment should the people remain unrepentant. Jesus warns that urgency is needed for the church because if they continue this loveless ministry, He will remove their lampstand from His presence (Rev. 2:4–5).

I don't know about you, but I struggle to find a single thing worse than Jesus removing me from His presence. This is essentially being cast into hell, a place absent from the presence of God. No thank you, I'll humble myself and repent no matter how many tears I may shed and how big of a shot my pride may take.

Should a church decide to not heed this warning given nearly two thousand years ago, the building and people may continue to exist physically, but they would become a spiritually dead church removed from Christ and without the empowerment of the Holy Spirit. Their actions would become a lesson in futility, as they would lack the anointing that would impact the world around them in any meaningful way—unless they repented.

Sadly, I have been a part of churches devoid of Holy Spirit power, and please believe me when I tell you, it takes a toll on you. My wife and I were called to one church, and we did try to have as positive an impact and be as Christlike as possible, but it was very, very difficult for us. There were certainly times we allowed ourselves to moan about our situation, and instead of focusing on the here and now, we would allow ourselves to dream of a day when we could take part in Spirit-inspired worship again. The only problem was we should have been focused on where God had us at that point in time.

As Jesus continues His letter, we see a classic case of "hate the sin, not the sinner."

Jesus mentions the deeds of the Nicolaitans, a group influenced by the ancient god and adversary Baal and his baalim.[1] Baal brought battles against Israel and turned the people of Israel against the God of Abraham, and he continues to bring battles against the church to this very day. Jesus, knowing all this, hates this spirit and the deeds his followers commit.

Fortunately for the church at Ephesus, they too hate the actions of the Nicolaitans, and while they do not receive a commendation for this (you are not supposed to tolerate sin), Jesus does affirm they are correct in their hatred of the Nicolaitans' deeds, knowing they are Baalic in origin (v. 6).

If you take the time to study the parts of the Old Testament that talk about the actions of those who worship Baal—child sacrifice, ritualistic mutilation, rites of sexual fertility, and many more demonic practices—you will see that the modern version of these ancient rituals is still very much alive today.

Lastly, Jesus calls the attention of all who receive this message and heed His warning: The tree God shut up from Adam and Eve will be made available again, granting the life originally planned for in God's great design.

> He who has an ear, let him hear what the Spirit says to the churches. To him who overcomes I will give to eat from the tree of life, which is in the midst of the Paradise of God.
> —REVELATION 2:7

As Jesus ends this letter to the Ephesian, or loveless, church, He speaks again to the unity and completeness of the Trinity. He commands those listening to hear what the Spirit says to the church, and Jesus Himself is the Word who has the power and authority to make available the tree of life found within the paradise of God the Father.

Three in One, One in Three.

SMYRNA: THE CANCELED CHURCH

Next, Jesus addresses one of two churches that have held to His tenets: the persecuted church in Smyrna. I like to think of

Smyrna as the canceled church. They have faithfully stood by the teachings of Jesus and have suffered for it.

This letter also sheds light on the coming persecution of churches within the United States.

Smyrna was a wealthy land,[2] much like America, that was spiritually poor. The church in Smyrna, however, was financially poor but alive spiritually and storing up for themselves treasures in heaven!

That takes faith rooted in Jesus Christ.

They lived in a land consumed with materialism (sound familiar?), and when a culture worships *things*, it is even harder for them to choose Jesus over a cancel culture that is after those who are faithful to the Lord. But Jesus was the cornerstone for the church in Smyrna, and thus they were able to endure the persecution.

As Jesus addresses this faithful church, He yet again establishes His authority to the angel of Smyrna:

> And to the angel of the church in Smyrna write, "These things says the First and the Last, who was dead, and came to life: 'I know your works, tribulation, and poverty (but you are rich).'"
>
> —Revelation 2:8–9

When you look at the words of Christ to the church, there is a sense of reassurance and rejuvenation in Jesus' acknowledgment of their suffering, something that is to be expected in the Christian walk.

To know the Lord is there and sees one's faith would give anyone the strength to continue on and push forward with building the kingdom of God in the face of persecution.

Jesus goes on to reference the Jews who have fallen away from faith (v. 9), much like the Pharisees who persecuted Him and no longer honored the Law of Moses but were instead plagued by a religious spirit. Jesus personally knows what the Smyrna church was enduring because He experienced it as well, to the point of death!

Persecution such as this is alive and well in the world today. It's not just from those who have nothing to do with Judeo-Christian values, but it's from many who think they are followers of Jesus but are completely absent of His radical love.

Spirits of religion, hard-heartedness, and haughtiness plague the Christian church today. They are the ones who wag their fingers in people's faces and cast judgment on anyone they come across. Meanwhile, as they are picking the specks out of the eyes of others, they are completely oblivious to the planks sticking out of their own.

It is actions and attitudes like these that have driven many away from the church before they even made it through the doors! They see these religious people who condemn anyone who operates in a manner different from their own, and they decide they want nothing to do with it.

These are the same people who persecuted the church at Smyrna—the ones who just know better and cannot be told anything because they simply cannot be wrong or mistaken.

Despite these efforts from those who were actively working against the church of Jesus, He shares with Smyrna the events and persecutions that were going to afflict them but tells them not to be afraid (v. 10). Being given this knowledge ahead of time allowed them, and future churches of Smyrna who abide in Christ, to take solace in the fact that Jesus would be with them every step of the way. These events would be used for the glory of God, and He had a plan and purpose in place, and they played an active role in that plan.

Having endured trials like this Himself, as He was tempted by Satan personally and still overcame the devil and his fiendish plans, Jesus gives a solemn objective: "Be faithful unto death, and I will give you the crown of life" (Rev. 2:10, ESV).

Who knows death better than Jesus? He holds the keys to it! Jesus suffered for three days and overcame death, giving Him the authority to grant others the crown of eternal life.

Jesus is not asking the church at Smyrna to do anything He Himself did not already do.

Honestly, as we read through the churches listed in Revelation, I see an aspect of each one in the church in America today. I am sure Christians around the world would agree with the state of their churches as well, but being an American and involved in Christian media, I am going to comment only on the state of the American church here.

PERGAMOS: THE COMPROMISED CHURCH

The church in Pergamos compromised in their faith. It is not that they were not still standing firm in Jesus, which He says they were, but they dropped their guard against the wiles of the enemy.

To the angel of Pergamos, Jesus reminds this watcher based in the seat of Roman power for the province[3] that He is still in control and prepared for war.

Paganism filled the area, and the church eventually allowed some of it to infiltrate their hearts.

This very thing is happening in America today. Witchcraft, the occult, New Age, idolatry, and sexual immorality of all kinds have all taken up residence in American society, as they are now broadcast across all media forms to children, youth, and adults.

From movies and magazines to the White House and video games, nearly every form of entertainment or social arena is influenced by witchcraft, the occult, and pagan rituals.[4]

But there are still Christians in the country who stand for the name of Jesus, although they have allowed the enemy in through the front door. Maybe they watch Disney movies that try to disguise occult practices, which God finds abominable, or they have tolerated sexual immorality taking place within their church community and failed to confront it. Whatever the reason, there are many churches across the nation in this very state of spirituality.

Much like the church today, the works of the church in Pergamos for the Lord were seen, something we must never doubt (God sees it all), but the commendation is kept relatively brief. Jesus acknowledges their faith in Him amid fierce persecution, including the death of one of the faithful, Antipas, who was martyred (v. 13).

Then, He addresses the sin that He has against them: They caved on doctrines that the Lord will not tolerate in His church.

> But I have a few things against you, because you have there those who hold the doctrine of Balaam, who taught Balak to put a stumbling block before the children of Israel, to eat things sacrificed to idols, and to commit sexual immorality. Thus you also have those who hold the doctrine of the Nicolaitans, which thing I hate.
> —REVELATION 2:14–15

Just how seriously does God take these sins? Well, to firmly and definitively answer this question, turn to Scripture.

By reading both the Old and New Testament verses that have to do with how God views idolatry and sexual immorality, it opens a window into His righteousness. We can see what these sins are and why God abhors them. In turn Jesus will not allow such sins to take place in His church either.

Satan knows how to be an effective infiltrator, and this is demonstrated by the fact that the church in America today is suffering from the same contagion of sin the Pergamos church also allowed.

Too often church leadership does not even address idolatry

in services. What are people putting before God? What are modern versions of carved images? The things that have replaced God are many in America, such as spending hours upon hours on our smartphones and social media apps while our Bibles gather dust and Bible-reading apps remain unopened.

Digital or physical, the Word is the Word, and we will not be able to access its life-changing power unless we spend time in it.

Now, for the sensitive topic, but in reality it's the topic God is quite passionate about yet too many pastors refuse to touch with a ten-foot pole: sexual immorality.

It's almost too easy for a Christian to point toward homosexuality and the entire LGBTQ movement and ideology and shoehorn that into being the current definition of sexual immorality, which, according to the Word of God, it is.

But do not think for a second that heterosexual immorality is not included in this as well.

For too long pastors and parents have stopped pushing abstinence and instead have gone along with the world in practicing safe sex. The safest and most righteous act is abstinence.

I fail to recall the last sermon I attended that warned and instructed me on what godly sexual morality was. We barely hear it these days, and I do not mean a finger-wagging, "you'll burn in hell if you mess up" message. I'm talking about really teaching people how Christians should behave between the sheets!

Are our youth prepared to go off to college, where they will become surrounded by sexual encounters? Are single adults, who may have remained single or been divorced or widowed, strong enough in their faith to resist the temptation of an act they have already taken part in?

On the surface these may seem like silly questions because the world is saturated with sex. It is everywhere, but the Bible is explicitly clear on how God views sexual immorality. It is such a major sin to Him that it is worthy of Jesus addressing a church that is taking part in it as a portion of the Revelation.

Paul also writes that the sexually immoral will not inherit the kingdom of heaven (1 Cor. 6:9–11). Can you imagine how much God despises the misuse of our bodies to have this message included in His Word to His creation? He abhors it! Yet churches have made an allowance for it, some to greater extents than others, but sin is sin and is not graded on a curve. If it is present, it must be removed and repented of, no exceptions.

Satan, meanwhile, loves it. He filled pagan temples with prostitutes, and the Jezebel spirit has pushed lust onto the world for thousands of years (but more on that later). And it is so easy for people to fall into the sexual lusts of the flesh, as the church in Pergamos found out.

They were established on the rock of Jesus, but being in such a pagan area rife with prostitution, they succumbed to their flesh. They proclaimed Jesus with their mouths, as He commends them for doing; they still clearly believed in Him. But then they left church and were devoured by the pagan practices of their land!

Christians must be stronger and more disciplined than that or we will eventually fall like the church at Pergamos did.

Thankfully, even in our sin Jesus offers us the opportunity to repent of our sins and be washed clean by the blood of the Lamb. Jesus is keenly aware of unrepented sins, and He remembers the sins of the Nicolaitans again as He warns the Pergamos church.

People really, really need to wake up to the fact that God hates sin. This is the second time He warns a church against paganism, also something He despises and that goes against the Ten Commandments, and sexual immorality. The two sins go hand in hand.

While the Lord is long-suffering and patient with us—and thank God for that, or I would be in some deep trouble—He has little patience for these pagan-related sins and will snuff out the church unless the church experiences true repentance and rejects fleshly living.

This very warning applies to the state of America as well.

We have opened the door to paganism[5] as we slammed the door on God. We worship idol images of celebrities on our smartphones, and we worship those phones more than anything else. Graven images are now spread far and wide across the country, while sexual immorality of all kinds has permeated every corner of culture and media.

America would do well to heed the words of Jesus, because He does not give them idly.

The blessings for those who reject the allure of idolatry and sexual immorality and who turn back toward the Lord and His heart are quite unique.

> To him who overcomes I will give some of the hidden manna to eat. And I will give him a white stone, and on the stone a new name written which no one knows except him who receives it.
> —REVELATION 2:17

Jesus promises the manna that sustained Israel and allowed them to continue their journey to God's Promised Land. The white stone is the acquittal of their sins and Christ's assurance that their turning to pagan gods would be forgiven. To Jesus these are grave sins, but in Jesus we will receive a new name and destiny, just as it happened for Jacob when he became Israel.

One thing that should be settling into a person's mind and spirit as they read these words of Jesus is that He is deadly serious. As we move on to the church and angel of Thyatira, we see the stance Jesus takes when confronting the spirit of Jezebel and those who follow in her footsteps. Death, and only death, awaits them.

Perhaps there are times when we as Christians focus entirely on the loving aspect of Jesus, which is wondrous and a point of His being that should be embraced wholeheartedly. But Jesus is multifaceted. He is the Lion and the Lamb, the Alpha and the Omega. He was there at creation, and He is going to bring about the end of the current era of creation. He is the rider on a white horse, and not just any type of horse, but a warhorse.

Isn't it amazing to see that each time Jesus addresses a church, after He establishes His lordship and authority, He builds up the church and always highlights what they are doing right?

How reassuring is that? Even in our sin, the Lord knows we are trying and working to serve Him, even when we sail off course over time.

THYATIRA: THE CORRUPT CHURCH

The corrupt church of Thyatira was caught in a trap very similar to the compromising church of Pergamos: sexual immorality and idolatry.

Jesus discusses eating the food of "things sacrificed to idols" (v. 20). This has a literal and metaphorical background, and while the literal is pretty self-explanatory, I would like to focus on the other part.

We have idol worship in our society today. Have you noticed some of the more modern "art" that has taken up residence in America?

The Arch of Palmyra,[6] which was re-created after the original was destroyed by ISIS, served as the entryway to the temple of Baal and took up residence in New York City and Washington, DC, during its worldwide tour.

Following that spiritual black eye, New York City saw a golden goddess ascend and take her place on the city's courthouse. According to the artist, Pakistani American Shahzia Sikander, this statue is representative of the "resistance" displayed by former Supreme Court Justice Ruth Bader Ginsburg. She also revealed it is a representation of the fight for abortion in America, of which she is a major proponent.[7]

So yes, idolatry has become a major issue in America today.

Abortion is idolized; celebrities with rabid fan bases are worshipped (look no further than a Taylor Swift concert if you do not believe me); sports teams see people spend more time following them than spending time with God. This list goes on and could be a book in and of itself. But make no mistake about it—this warning to the church at Thyatira is just as relevant for America today as it was for the physical church back then.

And who does Jesus identify as the corrupter of this church? The spirit of Jezebel (v. 20).

Many have heard of Jezebel before, but this evil spirit's name is not necessarily taken as seriously as she may have been at one time.

You've probably heard a story about some of the more conservative and older members of a rather strict denomination admonishing a younger female, perhaps even going so far as calling her a Jezebel.

I cannot stress enough the dangers of speaking such a thing over someone and opening a spiritual door into their life for such an evil spirit.

Just how bad is the Jezebel spirit? Well, Jesus gives us a preview of what is going to be coming her way later in the Revelation, but let's look at a couple of verses from what Jesus describes is going to happen to the children of Jezebel (those who follow her):

> And I gave her time to repent of her sexual immorality, and she did not repent. Indeed I will cast her into a sickbed, and those who commit adultery with her into great tribulation, unless they repent of their deeds. I will kill her children with death, and all the churches

shall know that I am He who searches the minds and hearts. And I will give to each one of you according to your works.
—REVELATION 2:21–23

Let us not leave room for any confusion in what Jesus is saying here: If you are a follower of Jezebel who commits sexual immorality, physically and spiritually, then you will die at the very hands of Jesus. That is how serious sexual immorality is to the Trinity.

These churches being led astray by sexual immorality also show just how powerful the allure of the flesh is.

This is the same spirit that led away the likes of Samson, a judge of Israel; that controlled the reign of King Ahab; and that has infiltrated and corrupted America. Lust disguised as love has taken up residence in the heart of the church, but lust being love could not be further from the truth.

Love is defined by the apostle Paul:

> Love suffers long and is kind; love does not envy; love does not parade itself, is not puffed up; does not behave rudely, does not seek its own, is not provoked, thinks no evil; does not rejoice in iniquity, but rejoices in the truth; bears all things, believes all things, hopes all things, endures all things.
> —1 CORINTHIANS 13:4–7

If you have any confusion on what actions, words, or thoughts fall under ways that *parade* themselves, are *puffed up*, are *iniquity*, and are provocative or *evil*, look no further than the Word of God and what it describes these actions as, and what God describes as righteous.

A deeper knowledge and understanding of the Bible will lead to greater discernment of the deception Satan tries to pass off as godly. Looking at society through a biblical lens is an eye-opening and quite shocking experience due to the sheer amount of warfare being fought in our world.

Deception is a strength of Jezebel, disguising the lusts of the flesh and purposefully misleading souls into a false love. These falsehoods open the way for many, as Americans have increasingly seen in the past few decades, to accept various forms of sexual immorality into their lives, such as homosexuality, incest, polygamy, and other unnatural and ungodly acts, as well as false relationships.

The spirit of Jezebel is a plague, infecting those who lay with her both spiritually and physically to date. The spread of sickness and disease through sexual immorality affects the world to this very day. Even as modern medicine tries to combat it, it continues to ravage people, yet many refuse to alter their lifestyles, and they simply accept these infirmities.

There is a path of redemption for these people, however, but any false repentance will be exposed through Christ's judgment. People cannot hide lustful actions from the righteous judge, and He will expose them.

Tragically, we have seen this affect not just society but Christian leaders of the highest caliber, men and women who were seemingly above reproach, yet God knew their hearts. These leaders who have succumbed to the flesh have caused immense harm to the church of Jesus Christ, but nothing, especially not the Jezebel spirit, will be able to destroy her.

Those who resist, however, as Jesus explains to the church of Thyatira, will receive an amazing reward: the morning star Himself (Rev. 2:26-28). They will earn this through true repentance and persevering through the persecution that will come their way for holding fast to the principles of Jesus.

Whenever I hear the name of Jesus being "the morning star," I am always reminded of what Satan lost.

He was the son of the morning, the son of the dawn, and so great was his splendor he once held. But this glory instead will now be given to the sinless subjects of Jesus. This placement was taken from Lucifer when he attempted to raise himself higher than Jesus, the morning star. So great was his fall and so devastating that his gift of being the son of the morning has been held, waiting for those who are worthy to be called such and given the gift of Jesus. Only when Satan's corruption and sin is defeated forever will the gift of the morning star be fully revealed in His glory.

CHAPTER 3

The DEAD, the FAITHFUL, and the LUKEWARM

JOHN'S WRITING CONTINUES Christ's direct messages to the churches, calling them to account for their deeds, warning them of impending judgment, and offering promises to those who overcome. In Revelation 3 the risen Lord exhorts Sardis, Philadelphia, and Laodicea, exposing spiritual deadness, commending steadfast faith, and rebuking lukewarm complacency, urging each to repent and walk in the fullness of His kingdom.

SARDIS: THE DEAD CHURCH

Revelation 3 begins with a reminder that the dead church of Sardis should never forget: Jesus holds them in the palm of His hand. He is God, and He sent the Holy Spirit to them as a helper, the One who empowers the elect. They must utilize the power of the Holy Spirit to stay alive and serve Him; otherwise, they would fail in spreading an effective gospel and defeating the spiritual enemy. Without the Holy Spirit they'd have no bite, no power.

Christ must be taken more seriously by this church, and let me tell you, the absolute same is true for the American church.

Cessationism is poison to the American church and deadens those who are caught in its grip. You can have the best Bible teacher in the world, but if they do not have the power of the Holy Spirit, they will not change the world around them. We are seeing this as denomination after denomination falls by the wayside, and the church members in them, while many are good people, are not growing the kingdom of God.

But not those who are filled with the Holy Spirit.[1] No, as a matter of fact those congregations are growing because people are seeing and experiencing the manifest presence of the Holy Spirit.

People are experiencing transformation, lives abundant with the power of the Holy Spirit behind them, and this is the exact opposite of a dead church. It is a church that wants more and more of Jesus and the outpouring of the Spirit, so they do what the Bible commands them to do: They fast in prayer and supplication; they engage the world around them in ministry with the love of Jesus leading the way; they engage in the gifts of the Spirit and verify them against the Scriptures (including weeding out the false messengers who seek to make a quick buck at the expense of the name of Jesus). They actually grow the kingdom; they are alive!

There are certainly churches like this across America and the world. But there must be more. Sadly, many are unwilling to resuscitate their dead churches, as they are caught up in the spirit of religion and haughtiness and refuse to take an introspective look into their own hearts and seek the changes the Lord wants to implement in their lives.

This is not always an easy process, to be sure. It is a humbling experience that often brings with it growing pains, tears, and a massive shot to our pride. Yet it is always worth it because we grow deeper and deeper into our relationship with God.

That is what Jesus is calling the dead churches of Sardis to do: to remove these dead practices and ceremonies and repent (Rev. 3:3). Then, they must strengthen themselves in the Holy Spirit so they can not only endure the world but overcome it! This means they cannot tolerate the worldly practices and ways that deaden them spiritually, for the love of the world (and themselves and their ideologies) leads only to death and spiritual impotence. A true, Spirit-filled, alive-in-Christ-Jesus church must prepare for discomfort, as the world will take notice of them, and the enemy will then target them in spiritual warfare.

Let's look at an interesting phrase, though, that Jesus says to the dead church.

Jesus says that because those who watch for His return are repentant and have not "defiled their garments" (or participated in pagan rituals and immorality), He "will not blot out [their] name[s] from the Book of Life" (vv. 4–5).

How long have people been arguing over the premise of losing salvation, also known as the "once saved, always saved" argument?

Far too often, spiritually immature people will say, "I repented and accepted Jesus," but then fail to change anything about themselves or their lifestyles.

But just look at the rewards Jesus promises the church at Sardis for its repentance! They are the Lord's righteousness and the certainty that their names will be written in the Lamb's Book of Life. With their robes they become new beings and pure as virgins as a part of the bride, and Jesus is their Bridegroom.

When God's ultimate judgment is passed, Jesus will read their names aloud for God and all heaven to hear. Their eternal life is assured, so says the King of kings.

PHILADELPHIA: THE FAITHFUL CHURCH

Next, Jesus addresses the church at Philadelphia, a city and church that lived up to its name's meaning of love.

This is the church that was the bride of Christ. These were the worshippers who, while imperfect, sought to grow in Christ daily, picked up their crosses, and strove to answer the call of the Great Commission.

We see elements of this church in our world today, but not nearly as much as we should. We see it in those who serve and seek no reward for themselves; they simply serve out of love and obedience to Jesus' commands. We see it in those who give faithfully, as Christians are to do, according to the Word of God. We see it in the churches that are empowered by the Holy Spirit and are changing their communities while growing the kingdom of God.

The description Christ gives to the church demonstrates His righteousness in all things, for He is holy as God is holy.

> These things says He who is holy, He who is true, "He who has the key of David, He who opens and no one shuts, and shuts and no one opens": "I know your works. See, I have set before you an open door, and no one can shut it; for you have a little strength, have kept My word, and have not denied My name."
> —REVELATION 3:7–8

When we read Jesus' opening words to the church, He exudes authority as the One who holds the key of David. He opens the door that no one can shut, and in turn He opens the door for His church to walk through as well. It is a door that the forces of hell have been unable to shut since Christ's victory over sin and death on the cross through His spilled, innocent blood and His resurrection three days later.

Jesus, the Seed of David who holds the key of David, possesses ultimate authority to command both the churches and the spiritual realms to which He speaks. With this authority, He alone determines which doors remain open for His church and which are shut, ensuring His sovereign will prevails.

The door leads to their blessing for keeping their faith. The faithful church must continue forward and walk through the door, but no one can close it (or take their salvation away). They have the strength, according to Jesus, to cross the threshold.

We also see another reference to a group of Jews (certainly not all Jewish people, of course; this is not an anti-Semitic diatribe) who were anti-Christian. They were holding to the tenets of Satan as opposed to the God of the patriarchs. They would reap what they sowed for attacking the Messiah's followers, whom He loves (v. 9). What an amazing thing, to have the Messiah include in God's Word that He specifically loves you, for all who read it to see!

Sadly, many use this verse and others in the Bible to attack God's chosen people, which is a folly of monumental proportions. The Abrahamic covenant (Gen. 12:1–3) is still in place and will be for as long as the current era lasts. There are many, many verses throughout the Old and New Testaments that demonstrate God's love for His people, before and after Jesus' victory on the cross.

For these faithful believers, however, He offers the reassurance of protection from what is to come (Rev. 3:10). He has this authority. No amount of persecution would turn this Philadelphia church, and we are beginning to see the worldwide spread of Christian persecution before our very eyes.

Christians in Nigeria are murdered by the thousands,[2] and the United Nations remains silent. Pastors in Canada are arrested for standing on biblical principles and speaking out against the perversions infecting their country.[3] America has all but abandoned the principles of God, which made this country great in the first place, and has instead embraced radical Marxist ideologies that have no place for God in them. Instead, the government becomes the people's god. Countries across Europe prosecute Christians who stand by the biblical principles of marriage, gender, and sexuality and even arrest those who silently pray outside abortion clinics.

How much longer before Christianity is outlawed altogether?

Yet even such radical legislation would not hinder the true church that is represented in Philadelphia.

The Dead, the Faithful, and the Lukewarm

Why? Because, as Jesus later says, those of the Philadelphia church, or the faithful church, would become as pillars in the temple of God (v. 12). And what does a pillar do? It holds up under immense weight, and without pillars a structure will not stand.

These faithful, these pillars, were able to withstand such pressure and weight. And it is a guarantee that they endured such pressure in the world because of their faithfulness.

It is a certainty that the world will actively target the faithful church, and the persecution will become increasingly worse. There are still those who think they can be passive in this spiritual war, and that is simply an outright falsehood. Lines will be drawn, and sides will be chosen. The enemies of Jesus will hunt down and try to ruin any who declare Jesus as Lord.

To withstand such an onslaught of persecution, the faithful church had deep, nourished roots in the Word of God, their personal relationships with Jesus Christ and each other in community, and the empowerment of the Holy Spirit. Without these things they would have been vulnerable like the other churches to which Jesus issues correction and offers the chance of repentance before His return.

The second coming of Jesus will be quick, and it is Jesus Himself who is warning us of this! "Behold, I am coming quickly! Hold fast what you have, that no one may take your crown" (v. 11). He is issuing a warning with this statement for the church because He does not want us to drop our guard or get complacent and miss out on it. The church must always be ready for His return, good and bad, and not let our love for Jesus grow cold. Instead, we must always keep and nurture that fire in our hearts until that glorious day.

It is on the backs of people like this that Jesus will build His temple in the New Jerusalem. Because, like the church, the temple of God is made up of the followers of Christ who will bring praise and adoration before the King. They are the pillars, honored by the One they came to honor.

Ending this letter to the church in Philadelphia, the faithful church, Jesus concludes with a statement that many contemplate to this day:

> I will write on him the name of My God and the name of the city of My God, the New Jerusalem, which comes down out of heaven from My God. And I will write on him My new name.
> —REVELATION 3:12

What is this *new name* Jesus refers to? Is He referencing a new name given to all those who enter into His eternal kingdom? Is He referring to a new name for Himself?

I like to entertain the thought that it is not necessarily a new name but a revealing of His eternal reigning name. People often point to the Bible verse in Hebrews 13:8, which reads, "Jesus Christ is the same yesterday, today, and forever."

That is absolutely true. But that does not mean this is not a name Jesus has had since the dawn of eternity and since God's plan for salvation came into being. He is the Alpha and Omega, who always was, is, and will be. So has the name of the eternal King not also been in existence just as long? It simply may not have been revealed. And let's be honest, God decides when and how He wants to reveal something.

Compound this with the fact that God has many, many names, as does Jesus. Yeshua, Jesus, Emmanuel, Bright and Morning Star, Jehovah, Yahweh, God—the list goes on and on. Having a name that is not yet revealed does not necessarily mean Jesus changes who and what He is. (Anyway, *Jesus* is the English way of saying His name, and the odds are we are not going to communicate with God in English when we get to heaven.)

Regardless of the many theories (mine included) on the matter it will be revealed in full at the timing of the Lord.

LAODICEA: THE LUKEWARM CHURCH

> These things says the Amen, the Faithful and True Witness, the Beginning of the creation of God: "I know your works, that you are neither cold nor hot. I could wish you were cold or hot. So then, because you are lukewarm, and neither cold nor hot, I will vomit you out of My mouth."
> —REVELATION 3:14–16

What an introduction to the lukewarm church—the church that Christ cannot stand and will spit out if they do not repent and change their hearts.

Jesus' names, "the Amen, the Faithful and True Witness, the Beginning of the creation of God," run parallel with what John wrote in his Gospel:

> In the beginning was the Word, and the Word was with God, and the Word was God. He was in the beginning with God. All things were made through Him, and without Him nothing was made that was made. In Him was life, and the life was the light of men.
> —JOHN 1:1–4

With authority Jesus declares that He always has been, always is, and always will be one with God and that His authority is divine and eternal.

Jesus' names bring truth to who He is, but they also show that what He says is the truth. This means people who read these words in Revelation must heed His words and warnings, or they simply will not survive.

Of any church to heed the warning of Jesus, I would think

this would be the one. To be threatened by the King of kings and Lord of lords that He will vomit you out due to your behavior as followers of His—that is a truly terrifying ultimatum.

Sadly, it also exemplifies the church today. Many are Christian in name only, and their hearts do not yearn for a deeper relationship with Jesus Christ.

Across America the "business" of having a church or ministry has made many men and women rich beyond their wildest dreams, but you will not feel an ounce of the Holy Spirit's presence in those places.

The rich back then in Laodicea, just like today, did not realize how much they needed God (Rev. 3:17). This is because they simply could not see past their worldly, material things and had become spiritually dead inside. That *thing* they knew was missing was Jesus Christ in their hearts, but they were unwilling to give up any physical comfort for spiritual renewal and restoration. The flesh, once it gets a grip on a person's heart, does not want to let go easily. That is why if you see someone experience true deliverance from a snare in life, they often weep deeply. The issue they have been dealing with snared their heart with spiritual hooks.

The Laodiceans' weak spirits could not see or discern the spiritual dryness affecting them, and Jesus is warning the church of this.

Simply going to church on Sunday, singing songs with no enthusiasm or true worship in the heart, and not spending any time in the Word of God during the week is a spiritual disease that has poisoned the American church. This lack of biblical knowledge and literacy has allowed for the church to become compromised in its convictions and yield to the principles and values of the world over the commandments of God.

We see it all around us. Many churches that bear the name of Jesus have replaced the cross with the pride flag, tolerate sin, and even promote it, all in the false teaching of tolerance.[4] Well, the Bible does not teach people to tolerate sin; in fact, it says the opposite. But do not get it twisted: We are absolutely to pray and intercede for the deceived and love the person.

But to tolerate sin? Absolutely not.

The American church for too long has become comfortable, and during that time, the roots of Satan's corruption were taking hold of every single aspect of society: the media, the arts, sports, cultural ideologies, the public school system from kindergarten to postgraduate courses, the military, and politics. Satan has worked to not only remove God from these aspects of society but make them hostile toward His principles and designs as well.

This corruption has worked only too well, as we have seen a fundamental change in America over the last several decades, one that is rejecting God, embraces satanism, and is run by those influenced and controlled by demons, principalities, and rulers of darkness. But Jesus tells John through the angel,

> As many as I love, I rebuke and chasten. Therefore be zealous and repent. Behold, I stand at the door and knock. If anyone hears My voice and opens the door, I will come in to him and dine with him, and he with Me.
> —REVELATION 3:19–20

If only every person who claims to be a follower of Jesus would heed this warning, offer up true repentance from their heart, and receive the baptism of the Holy Spirit. What an impact that would have on the nation and the world!

Jesus provides us with an example of what His true love is, and we can see two different aspects of that same love. He died on the cross and took upon Himself all the sins of humanity, suffering in ways no human can even fathom. Yet He is also rebuking those of the lukewarm church in love. Loving someone as Christ loves them does not mean you capitulate to their sinful lifestyle and go along with them. Jesus is offering loving correction because if He doesn't, they will know eternal death.

So what is the truly loving action? Is it tolerating sin and in some cases even encouraging it, or is it offering correction from a lifestyle that will see the person experience eternity in hell? I would pray someone who loved me would offer correction if I ever wandered off the path God has set before me.

Rewarding those who heed His word, Jesus says they will reign with Him and even sit with Him on His throne (v. 21).

Yet the church must overcome temptation and the world if it wants to sit on the throne of Jesus. He overcame sin and death to claim His rightful spot atop God's throne.

Jesus is knocking at the door of the lukewarm church's heart, but would they come back to Him and open it and, in doing so, become reunited with their first love? This will not be an easy process for those who do, as Jesus describes. For those who overcome, the obstacles in their paths will be love of money, love of self, comfort in the world, materialism, and indifference to their current spiritual state.

These letters to the seven churches and spirits all point to one thing: The sovereign reign of Jesus Christ is coming, and they must be prepared for it. If not, the consequences will be catastrophic and horrific beyond comprehension.

CHAPTER 4

The VISION of the THRONE

Now that Jesus has finished telling John what to write to the seven churches, the seven spirits, things take a turn. The Revelation given to John by the authority of God the Father shifts.

There are many different interpretations regarding the biblical prophecies we will encounter throughout this book. As stated in the introduction, this commentary is by no means a be-all, end-all, definitive answer to the mystery that is Revelation. The goal of this book is to point people to read the Word of God for themselves and to start conversations with one another about the end-times we are living in and to continue the Great Commission that all Christians are called to engage in.

John listened to Jesus in the Spirit. He listened to the Lord about the churches and the role he had in planting them as one of the twelve disciples who started the evangelistic ministry of Jesus Christ.

What John experienced next is a continuation of the revelation vision given to him by his Lord and Savior. Just imagine how being in heaven and the glory of the Lord is incomparable to being on earth. It is certainly something to think about, especially since the Bible discusses the intensity of the power of God.

> After these things I looked, and behold, a door standing open in heaven. And the first voice which I heard was like a trumpet speaking with me,

> saying, "Come up here, and I will show you things which must take place after this." Immediately I was in the Spirit. And there was a throne set in heaven with One sitting on the throne!
>
> —REVELATION 4:1–2

Now a similar but distinctly different heavenly voice is speaking to John. In the beginning of the Revelation, this is specifically attributed to Jesus Christ, but no longer. The red letters of our Lord have ceased, and now it appears to be one of the criers of heaven announcing the throne room of God the Father—arguably the most majestic sight in creation a being can view.

The One sitting on the throne is none other than God the Father, for Jesus is the Word, and the Word was with God in creation. Jesus, however, will also establish His throne in New Jerusalem, while God reigns forever in heaven. Even with a new heaven and earth, God's throne is exceptional. But we will get to the establishment of the new throne later in this book.

God the Father is showing John that which is to come, as is His authority to do. Even Jesus asserted that no one knows the hour or the day but His Father (Matt. 24:36). The logical step, then, is for the Father to continue the Revelation to John, for it is His and His alone to reveal.

Almost stunned by the brilliance of the throne room of heaven, John tries to find a way to describe the majestic glory that surrounds the Father's seat of power. Mere words cannot truly describe its awesomeness.

> There was a rainbow around the throne, in appearance like an emerald. Around the throne were twenty-four thrones, and on the thrones I saw twenty-four elders sitting, clothed in white robes; and they had crowns of gold on their heads. And from the throne proceeded lightnings, thunderings, and voices. Seven

lamps of fire were burning before the throne, which are the seven Spirits of God.

—REVELATION 4:3–5

Now things begin to get a little confusing for many, but fear not! The Bible contains many of the answers to your questions regarding the seven Spirits of God.

As for the twenty-four thrones and the twenty-four elders who are purified by God's righteousness and are in constant worship of God, there are absolutely no identifiers as to who these men are. And I say *men* as there are some who think they may be of angelic origin; I simply do not believe this to be so. But that is my opinion.

It is an entertaining imagination exercise to consider who these elders may be, because they must be of great righteousness, but it also begs a question: Are they all men, or would there be some women as well?

Now, I understand the Greek word *presbyteros* is in reference to older men who are able to rule over a church, and in this case they are representative of Christ's church. In the times John lived in, men were certainly the dominant leaders, but even Paul acknowledges the women in ministry who helped him along his journeys. In their respective churches, women were leaders, and one particular woman in the Bible sticks out in my mind as a possible member of this group of twenty-four elders. This group is representative of the church, and women are most assuredly an integral part of it, even though John makes no distinction in his writings.

That woman is Deborah.

The prophetess of ancient Israel, a judge, was the leader of Israel before they had earthly kings to lead them. This woman was so revered that Barak refused to go into battle without her. She oversaw the nation of Israel—after God, of course. She trusted in the Lord, even when the men were weak and faithless.

Much like David, in victory over their enemy Deborah and Barak sang praises to the Lord Most High. And to have a heart like David's is to have a heart for God.

Deborah was such an important figure that she has two entire chapters of the Bible written about her and the forty years of peace Israel saw under her leadership (Judg. 4–5). For such a peace to occur, the leadership must have been righteous, and what is the prevailing quality that would see someone chosen as one of the twenty-four elders? I would argue righteousness would be very high on the list.

This is all speculation, of course, but I certainly entertain the thought. If Deborah was a righteous prophetess, like Elijah was a prophet, and if she was a righteous leader of Israel like David (who certainly committed atrocious sins), then maybe, just maybe, she would be considered as one of the twenty-four who experience the glory, power, and majesty of the throne room of heaven.

But the time of knowing for certain is not yet, and it is more than a possibility that all the elders are, in fact, all men of righteousness.

Regardless, in John's writings the elders are not identified. (I would love it if one of them were Billy Graham; I feel like that is very fitting.) The crowns are given to them as rewards for their faithfulness, much like Jesus' rewards to the members of the churches who repent and continue to follow Him, even in the face of severe persecution. The thrones given to the elders encircle the throne of God, a reward in and of itself, to constantly be in the presence of the Father and His glory.

What an unbelievable experience that is.

The Throne Room

Think of the power and sound of lightning and thunder on the earth. How much greater and more terrifying, in a holy way, is the Lord's glory manifested as lightning and thunder in the throne room?

The Spirits of God are represented, and many are confused by this portion—I know I was. Let's clear something up: There is only one Holy Spirit who is a part of the Trinity—Father, Son, and Holy Spirit. He is not split up into seven other beings. Look to Isaiah 11:2 to read about what exactly the seven Spirits are, or should I say the seven characteristics of the one Holy Spirit.

> There shall come forth a Rod from the stem of Jesse, and a Branch shall grow out of his roots. The Spirit of the LORD shall rest upon Him, the Spirit of wisdom and understanding, the Spirit of counsel and might, the Spirit of knowledge and of the fear of the LORD.
> —ISAIAH 11:1–2

Each of these traits of the Holy Spirit is represented by the seven lamps around the throne.

No description that John gives can truly relay the awesomeness of what he saw, but he still does a really good job of it all. John would have been overwhelmed in the physical, which is why he had to be taken up in the Spirit.

When reading through this part of Revelation 4, it almost begs the question: How was John not overwhelmed by all this? Being in the Spirit was the only thing allowing him to experience the inner throne room of God! The things he saw—the elders, the thrones, the lamps, not to mention the angelic beings—must have been absolutely overwhelming.

Speaking of the angelic beings, the creatures John saw are angels (vv. 6–8). The awe of seeing inside the holy of holies must have been astounding to John. This was a different level of relationship he had entered. He had an earthly and spiritual relationship with the Son and a relationship with the Holy Spirit at Pentecost and afterward. Now he was invited to witness the Revelation at the throne of the Father—to see mighty angels and elders with authority bow down, worship, and glorify the God of all things in His sanctum.

These beings and elders are established for the very task that God wants humans to choose for themselves: to worship Him!

Here is a little breakdown I came up with studying their words of worship before the Lord in verses 8 and 11:

- **"Holy, holy, holy"**: God's divinity as *the* Holy One. His holiness and righteousness are so great He cannot, and will not, tolerate sin in His presence or domain. Thus, when Lucifer committed the "original sin," he was cast out of heaven as though a bolt of lightning struck. This culmination of the current era ends with the total and final eradication of sin at the hands of God's perfect sacrifice: Jesus Christ.

- **"Lord God Almighty"**: praise of His great power over all things. As the Creator, He has power and authority over all things that ever were, are, and will be. He controls time and space while the very existence of creation bends to His will.

- **"Who was and is and is to come"**: God simply is. Humans are mentally incapable, in physical form, of comprehending eternity. God always has been, an eternity of eternities that is not able to be calculated. And He always will be. There is no end to Him, His reign, His authority, or His power. It will always be. Along with God the Father is the Word, who was there at the beginning with Him and took human form to overcome sin and death while redeeming mankind in the process. Wherever one finds the Father, you find the Son and the Holy Spirit.

- **"You are worthy, O Lord"**: God is justice, power, and righteousness. His purity, power, and wisdom justify Him being worthy of all praise, for no one person or thing is or ever will be like God. Lucifer deceived himself into thinking it was possible for him to rival God's greatness. By doing this, he has paid the price by receiving the worst punishment imaginable: becoming the enemy of God.

- **"To receive glory and honor and power"**: These three things are given freely to the Lord by His creation. Mankind, the beings God created in His own image, freely gives God the glory in all things, for He has power over all things. He is given honor from His subjects, for He loves them greatly but holds them accountable for their actions according to His standards and principles. Love does not mean withholding correction, but enforcing it. So great is this love, in fact, that He sent Jesus Christ, the Word made flesh, to be the sacrificial Lamb who would cover the sins of all humanity. God is all-powerful—make no mistake—but He gave mankind the power of free will. Yet by being given this gift of choice, as Adam and Eve chose to sin against God in the Garden of Eden, humans can choose to give back to God the power over their lives and walk the path He has set before them, thus living life in God's will and not their own. By doing so, they honor Him and give Him glory and power in the successes and accomplishments in their lives.

- **"For You created all things":** This is an acknowledgment of God's omnipotence and praise for His great power. His power to create all things justifies His lordship over said creation, making Him worthy to receive praise from that very creation. Without Him there would be no existence, no purpose, nothing. It was His unlimited power, on a scale that is unimaginable, that allowed creation to take place—to form the universe we live in and the earth we live on, to have every molecule and atom stabilized and formed down to the most minute detail. The very system of the human body is of a design so remarkable we have not fully unlocked the secrets within it. That is how powerful, intelligent, and imaginative our God truly is.

- **"And by Your will they exist and were created":** All creation in the physical realm came into being because God wanted it. Every single iota of existence is because God desired it. God wanted every single human being to be in relationship with Him. He gave each one the choice to choose Him or reject Him, but there are dire consequences for rejecting our Creator. To choose sin is not just a rejection of God; it is choosing a life completely devoid of His presence, which is literally hell.

This look into the throne room, which God granted John to have, in turn gives us a unique perspective of what God desires: worship.

This life, our creation, is not about us; it's about *Him*! We are bombarded with so many self-gratifying and self-aggrandizing promotions in every aspect of media and culture today that we lose sight of how we are commanded to live in the Bible, which is selflessly.

We are to put God first and His ways before our own. This is evident by the worship given to Him in His throne room by the great angelic beings and the twenty-four elders. When we magnify His holy name and lift Him up in praise, He in turn lifts us up and draws us closer into relationship with Him. That is far greater than anything the world can offer us.

CHAPTER 5

The LAMB UNSEALS the SCROLLS

THE TONE OF the Revelation shifts back to John, who again identifies himself while he views God the Father holding the scroll that only One is worthy of opening.

We need to realize what a great and important event this is, for it is proclaimed throughout the heavens, a search for the One and only One worthy to open the scroll.

John is aware enough to recognize the strength of the angel before God's throne. This angel acts as the herald of the Lord, using its booming voice to search for the One to open the seals of the scroll of God (Rev. 5:2–3). To accomplish this task, this being must be God's equal and have His authority.

No one but the One has accomplished this. By becoming the perfect sacrifice, the conqueror of sin and death, and shedding His blood on the cross and being raised from the dead on the third day, Jesus earned this right, this authority, this justification to take hold of the scroll and open it.

If you've ever heard the old hymn, "There is pow'r, pow'r, wonder-working pow'r in the precious blood of the Lamb,"[1] well, that is one of the truest statements you'll ever hear.

Use this power of the blood in prayer and spiritual warfare, because it is this precious blood that overcame sin and death, and no power of hell can stand up to it.

John continues,

> So I wept much, because no one was found worthy to open and read the scroll, or to look at it. But one of the elders said to me, "Do not weep. Behold, the Lion of

the tribe of Judah, the Root of David, has prevailed to open the scroll and to loose its seven seals."
—REVELATION 5:4–5

Now, before the elder reassures him, John must have believed that Jesus could have opened the scroll, but his writing explains that no one is worthy. Perhaps he incorrectly assumes Jesus is a part of those who are deemed unworthy and unable to open the seals.

This potential, momentary idea that Jesus could not, in fact, open the seal is a devastating thought that causes John to weep not only for mankind but for himself. His faith is shaken at this thought, for he gave Jesus his everything! The sheer thought of making a mistake in his faith, seeing all his fellow disciples suffer and at times die for Christ, overwhelms his spirit.

But it is not to remain this way.

When one of the elders reassures John that there is, in fact, One worthy—the Lion of the tribe of Judah and the Root of David (which Jesus already identified as Himself)—it is in a kind and possibly familiar manner. Perhaps this is a prophet of old who knows of John's work and faith as one of Jesus' handpicked disciples, or an even closer person to John. Perhaps it is, in fact, one of the Twelve who has been granted the honor of being one of the twenty-four elders who encircle the throne of God. Even wilder—and please understand this is all speculation but within the realm of possibility—perhaps it is his own brother, James.

What a trip that would be, seeing your own earthly brother who died by the sword at the hand of King Herod elevated to one of the highest positions in the kingdom of God, in the throne room no less!

But alas, we won't know any of these things for certain until we are with Him.

I don't know about you, but I will have so many questions for the Lord when I finally arrive before Him.

But I digress. John is so reassured by the words of the elder, he stops weeping and annotates it in the final book of the Bible. He knows everything is going to be OK as Jesus assumes control of the scroll of God.

Even in a dream or a vision in the Spirit, a person may have an emotional reaction to what is happening before them.

THE VISION OF THE LAMB

Amid everything taking place, including being in the throne room itself, John sees the Lamb.

The figure who is central to all God's plans for creation and the redemption of all mankind—Jesus is at the center of it all. The Word who was with God at the beginning. The Omega who will be there for all eternity. He is always mentioned between the Father and the Spirit. The core. He is the bridge for humanity to cross and enter into the Father's presence. He is the One who will ride His horse into battle and defeat the devil, God's ancient enemy, once and for all.

With the elder's explanation—the Lion of Judah and Root of David—John knows this Lamb to be his Messiah. He recognizes his Savior and the wound John had personally seen on His body: "In the midst of the elders, stood a Lamb as though it had been slain, having seven horns and seven eyes, which are the seven Spirits of God sent out into all the earth" (v. 6).

This description of the Lamb, with His seven horns and seven eyes, demonstrates John's incredible spiritual discernment by identifying the seven Spirits of God and of the one Holy Spirit, which we previously discussed. With this second mention of those same Spirits, however, I would highly encourage you to read over Isaiah 11.

The Lamb Unseals the Scrolls

Actually, read all of Isaiah because it is just that good and eye-opening!

John watches as his faith in Jesus is rewarded before his very eyes! He is rewarded with direct, visual confirmation that Jesus, the Lamb, is the Son of God that He always said He was. (And John firmly believed this, but to have something so assuredly confirmed for a believer is a whole new level of faith.) He watches as Jesus approaches the throne of God and is handed the scroll from the Father's hand (v. 7).

Who else but Jesus could do this? The simple answer is no one.

For John, seeing this interaction of the Father and the Son before death took John's spirit is an event exclusive to him, and him alone. He has definitive knowledge of the throne and Jesus' interaction with, and His authority before, the Father.

Watching in awe of what is taking place before him, John sees the Lamb assume control of God's scroll, His command, His will, His orders and plan for creation's end, and its new eternal beginning. The angelic creatures and elders recognize Jesus' authority as God's authority and bow down in worship, holding up an offering of the prayers of the redeemed before the risen Lord (v. 8).

It is in the worship of the elders that, again, I believe they were once men who have been elevated by God to be rulers in His throne room.

Revelation 5:9 says, "And have redeemed us to God by Your blood out of every tribe and tongue and people and nation" (MEV).

This leads me to believe that they were personally led to God by the bridge Jesus created with His perfect sacrifice. They hail from all over the world, and perhaps from different time periods of the world as well, but are found righteous before the Lord.

As the beings of worship proclaim the worthiness of Jesus in the middle of God's throne room—something that would only be done for the One who was an equal of God in authority and holiness (and as Jesus said, He is of the Father, and the Father is of Him)—John notices the landscape around him has changed.

All heaven has joined the angelic beings and elders in the throne room to celebrate and worship the eternal King of kings and Lord of lords (vv. 11–12).

This reverence shown to the Father is now also given to Jesus, who claimed victory over sin and death. It demonstrates the equal status, power, and authority over creation within the Trinity.

Somehow, perhaps through another example of supernatural discernment, John is able to know, see, or hear and understand that every creature from all creation joins in this praise of the Lamb (v. 13). They know the Lamb is about to start the end of existence as we know it by unsealing the scroll.

CHAPTER 6

The SEALS BROKEN

Now John witnesses the fantastic power and authority of Jesus Christ as He breaks the seals that begin God's judgment upon the earth.

Heeding the command of the angelic being, whose own power is great considering its station in heaven, John submits his own spirit to the authority granted to it and looks upon the conqueror, who will rule for a period of time.

THE FIRST SEAL

> I saw when the Lamb opened one of the seals....And I looked, and behold, a white horse. He who sat on it had a bow; and a crown was given to him, and he went out conquering and to conquer.
> —REVELATION 6:1–2

Some have theories that because this rider is on a white horse, it is in fact Jesus. However, I do not subscribe to these beliefs. This rider is all wrong for Jesus and His entrance on a white horse. This rider is going to oppress the people he conquers, not as a savior but as an authoritarian. We see evidence around us today of this type of totalitarian state that the conqueror will usher in.

Globalists are actively consolidating power and work tirelessly to strip away the remaining freedoms from the people of the world. By his own admission Yuval Noah Harari, author of *Sapiens: A Brief History of Humankind*, who has spoken at the World Economic Forum conference in Davos, Switzerland, said in a TEDx Talk,

> Human rights are just like heaven, and like God; it's just a fictional story that we have invented and spread around. It may be a very nice story. It may be a very attractive story; we want to believe it. But it's just a story; it's not a reality....The only place you find rights is in the fictional stories.[1]

Look, I'll be the first to say that for a long time, I did not believe those whom I considered conspiracy theorists about a "New World Order" or a threatening and sinister "One World Government." Yet as I look around at the world we live in today, I see the beginning stages of the world preparing for this first seal to break open and a conqueror to go forward and trample over the people of the world to make way for the Antichrist.

But what other events could throw the world into such chaos that it would carve out the path for a spirit of oppression through conquering the peoples of the world?

Well, one such potential event is the collapse of the United States as the lone superpower in the world.

Yes, people have said China rivals us, but the US, as of this time in 2025, is still so far ahead of China in terms of technology, development, military, and having the dollar as the world's foremost currency. I still view the US at the top alone.

That is probably why Russia, China, and the other members of the Brazil, Russia, India, China, and South Africa (BRICS) alliance have created a very real possibility of breaking the American dollar.[2]

This is a very powerful weapon of a political and economic nature that could end up oppressing people and conquering nations economically without a single shot being fired.

Having a bow as a weapon of choice is also unlike the description we read about the Warrior-King, Jesus Christ, who has a two-edged sword emerging from His mouth. Not to mention that the weapon of the Holy Spirit is the sword of the Spirit.

A bow is not a weapon that is in the thick of fighting the way a sword, axe, or mace is. It is a ranged weapon, wielded with precision and aim, much like the tactics needed to overthrow the world economy and potentially pave the way for the one-world currency of the Antichrist.

Here's a little personal theory for you, to explain why I do believe the dollar will be replaced and plunge the US into very tough times economically: The Antichrist would never use a monetary system that has for so long borne the words, "In God we trust."

Now, Satan is a corrupter, make no mistake about it, and he has, of course, corrupted money in the US to be its own god and idol to millions. But it still bears those words, and it has got to make him mad every single day that cash is still being used and people see those words on the money.

The devil must erase that financial system because for him this would be a perceived victory over believers in God who set Him over the money of the nation. But no matter how crafty the devil thinks he is, God has had this all planned out for all eternity. He knows the events of the world will lead to the Antichrist's system, and nothing happens without His allowance.

The Lamb, who was found worthy to open the scroll of God, continues breaking the seals to unveil the scroll in John's presence. John now knows that the horrors coming to the earth are necessary for Jesus' complete victory, but pain and suffering await those within the earthly realm.

The Second Seal

As the second seal breaks, and even now as I reread the verses, seeing how this is shaping in our world today, it is hard not to think that this rider is already at work in the world.

Being instructed by the second angelic being, John sees the rider in red who will take peace away from the earth (vv. 3–4). Remember what Jesus said in Matthew 24? That there will be wars and rumors of wars around the world? Never in my life—having lived through the end of the Cold War, the Gulf War, Kosovo, the genocide in Rwanda, a two-decade war in the Middle East, and a constant threat from China—have I seen the world in such a state of war as I have today.

And to think my grandparents lived through World War I, World War II, the Korean War, and Vietnam on top of what I listed!

Currently, and this is just a few of the conflicts taking place in the world, Israel is locked in a war with Hamas, Hezbollah, and several Iranian-backed proxy groups; Ukraine and Russia are still fighting; China has its eye on Taiwan; Fulani herdsmen are murdering Nigerian Christians by the thousands; and North Korea is always threatening the world when they feel like they are not getting enough attention.

This red rider, the one taking peace away from the earth, carries a "great sword," according to John (Rev. 6:4).

Now, *this* is a weapon, unlike the first rider's bow and arrow, that is meant to get in the face of its opponent and cleave them in two.

A large sword is an offensive weapon at its very core, but this rider will do more than bring war to remove peace from society. Just look at the vitriol in the protests from radical feminists, the Antifa thugs who use literal fascist tactics (the irony is amazing here), the deceived radical gender activists who take joy in mutilating the bodies of young children (including chemical castration), the abortion activists who worship their pagan gods with slaughtered babies, the news media who foam at the mouth whenever a Christian is elevated to a position of power, and the list goes on and on.

Cultures around the world are already at a place that is far from peace, and I firmly believe we are only in the beginning, preparatory stages of the end-times. Much more still needs to take place, and already the world feels as though it is on the brink of World War III, and no society has peaceful streets in the major cities.

The red rider, the taker of peace, is a good candidate behind the radical Islamist movement that has literally invaded Europe,[3] an invasion allowed by incompetent, ineffectual, and perhaps even demonically influenced leadership.

Peace can be stripped from economies as well, and a worldwide recession (or perhaps even a crash) would certainly do the trick of removing peace from investors and causing people of all industrialized countries to be fearful for their future when there is no certainty in the markets. But this will most likely come with the next rider, although that does not mean the disruption could not start when the second seal is broken.

Just imagine—pensions, gone. Retirements, gone. Social Security, no more. Inflation, raging. Debt, piling up. Foreclosures, historic. Groceries, unaffordable. The dollar, worthless.

Where would there be peace in this world besides the truth and promise of Jesus Christ?

We have the road map of what is to come. Are people getting ready spiritually, physically, and mentally?

The red rider will cause conflict in all aspects of society, even within the household, not just on the battlefield. Families, political parties, faith groups, sports teams—*all* aspects of society will be fractured. With the rider wielding this large sword we can expect murders and homicides to increase at an exponential rate, even more so than major cities are seeing now.

The Third Seal

As the next seal is broken by the Lamb, it is one that people have experienced a taste of in recent years.

During the early stages of the COVID-19 lockdowns, with trucking and shipping slowed, people saw a massive decline in products on store shelves.

I experienced this firsthand in a small suburb of Columbus, Ohio, not even in the major city. As people around the world were still wondering what was happening during the lockdown, toilet paper, paper towels, tissues, meats, bread, and much more were in short supply.

Getting to the closest grocery store one day for my weekly rounds, I decided to get there as the doors opened, only to find approximately fifteen to twenty others had that same idea as well. Remember, this is not a major city but a town about thirty minutes north of Columbus. I can only imagine the chaos of going to a New York City grocery store, or Los Angeles, or Chicago.

This rider, who will be released by the Lord and bring about scarcity in the world, will do so within a limited role (vv. 5–6). Even with these restraints people will turn on each other when supplies run thin.

We witnessed some of this ugliness in 2020, but this will drive humans to even deeper depths of evil. Remember, at this point the world will be full of those who are lovers of themselves. Few will have the tenets of the Lord and serve and think of others.

In the midst of this release another of the four living creatures at the throne bellows with authority given to it by God, instructing the rider what to do and in what capacity: "A quart of wheat for a denarius, and three quarts of barley for a denarius; and do not harm the oil and the wine" (v. 6).

Who grants such authority as this but the Father? The economic woes stemming from this rider will most likely dwarf any recession seen in human history.

THE FOURTH SEAL

It is truly difficult to comprehend the mayhem that is going to occur during the biblical end-times as the seals are broken, the trumpets are blown, and the bowls of God's wrath are poured out on the earth. Humanity has never seen anything like it, and chaos will ensue across the planet.

The pale rider, whose color is reminiscent of disease and pestilence, is granted the power of death over a set amount of the world, much like in Job's case. The devil was not allowed to kill Job and was restricted in what he was allowed to strike Job with, much like the rider is limited in the scale of how many will be killed by his hand.

But make no mistake, 25 percent of the earth's population will die in extraordinary circumstances.

> Behold, a pale horse. And the name of him who sat on it was Death....And power was given to them over a fourth of the earth, to kill with sword, with hunger, with death, and by the beasts of the earth.
> —REVELATION 6:8

As of today, 2025, the estimated world population sits at 8.2 billion people,[4] and a 25-percent extermination of humanity leaves 2.05 billion dead while the pale rider is at work in the world. That is simply unimaginable, as would be the impact of this loss of life.

Businesses, families, churches, governments, food production, the power grid, technology—every single aspect of the earth will feel the impact of this loss of life, and some of it coming from the beasts of the earth! What is that going to look like? How will the media cover those deaths? Dense population centers will become hot spots for crime (*sword*), and there will be empty shelves in stores (*hunger*), as well as sicknesses and illness (*death and disease*).

These four riders of the apocalypse appear to be unrighteous counterparts to the creatures before the throne who call out their appearances. Instead of worship before the Lord God, they bring with them widespread death, destruction, pain, and suffering.

THE FIFTH SEAL

Then, as Jesus continues by releasing the fifth seal, John beholds all who have given their lives for Christ as martyrs. Recognizing who they are must have shocked John, because he knew many who had died for the name of Jesus—even his own brother.

John also sees their special place at the part of the altar where the blood is collected during sacrifices to God (v. 9). He knows that even as they are blessed by the Lord with robes of purity, more have to join them at the altar. He knows things will get worse for the saints on the earth, but they will be met with justification and reward for their suffering.

Even as they cry out for the Lord's vengeance to rain down upon those who took their lives, God has them wait just a bit longer so that others may be saved (vv. 10-11).

Even as the world delves into darkness, God holds His ultimate judgment so that others may experience His loving mercy.

One thing Christians must understand—it is essential to get this—is that times of great persecution are coming for believers around the world. Yes, we all hope and pray for the outpouring of the Holy Spirit and for revival to sweep across the land, and it will. But these two events are not mutually exclusive. We can experience a great outpouring of the Holy Spirit in the very midst of persecution; in fact, many people throughout history have experienced this.

Indian Christians are constantly under threat in their country, yet the Holy Spirit is moving mightily there. The underground church in China flourished under the heavy-handed oppression of the Chinese Communist Party. Wherever Satan tries to snuff out the light and envelop the people in darkness, the light ends up shining even brighter.

This is simply not something American Christians have experienced to the degree other parts of the world have. We have been blessed beyond measure due to the Christian founding of this nation.

People to this day argue against this notion, that America was never a Christian nation, but I firmly disagree.

With the Great Awakenings, leadership honoring the Lord, and the Ten Commandments and Bibles adorning our government's halls and schools, America was a Christian nation in every aspect and enjoyed the blessing of being such.

THE SIXTH SEAL

John describes what happens when the sixth seal is opened:

> There was a great earthquake; and the sun became black…and the moon became like blood. And the stars of heaven fell.…Then the sky receded as a scroll… and every mountain and island was moved out of its place. And the kings of the earth, the great men, the rich men, the commanders, the mighty men, every slave and every free man, hid themselves in the caves and in the rocks of the mountains, and said to the

> mountains and rocks, "Fall on us…! For the great day of His wrath has come, and who is able to stand?"
> —Revelation 6:12–17

In whatever manner these events occur, it is going to be bad on earth. John sees the inhabitants flee at the might of the Lord and wish for death. But it is crazy to me that even in their fear, they are still unrepentant. How hard of a heart must one have, how spiritually deceived must one be, to still reject God after witnessing such devastation, prophesied in the Bible?

CHAPTER 7

The SEALED of ISRAEL

ALLOW ME TO start this chapter by prefacing with this: The seventh chapter in Revelation offers what I consider one of the most comprehensive examples in the Bible of God's covenant with Abraham, still in effect until the end of time.

For far too long now, far too many have believed in this absurd notion that the church of Christ has somehow replaced the nation of Israel.

We as Christians have been invited into the fold of salvation through the precious blood of Jesus Christ. But we who are Gentiles take no part in the Abrahamic covenant, which the Lord established with His servant Abram, who became Abraham.

There are promises, prophecies, and end-time events that must be fulfilled and take place with the nation of Israel—not the church of Christ, which includes Jews and Gentiles alike.

This discourse could, of course, take up a book in and of itself, but if you would like a quick read that does an excellent job of explaining to Christians the importance of the nation of Israel, read the article titled "A Christian's Relationship and Responsibility to Israel" by Pastor Greg Denham of Rise Church in San Marcos, California, which was published by *All Israel News*.[1]

Before John writes down those of Israel who are to be sealed away for the Lord (Rev. 7:4–8), he witnesses angels holding back even more tribulation that is intended for the earth.

> I saw four angels standing at the four corners of the earth, holding the four winds of the earth, that the wind would not blow on the earth or on the sea or on

> any tree. And I saw another angel ascending from the east, having the seal of the living God. He cried…"Do not harm the earth or the sea or the trees, until we have sealed the servants of our God."
>
> —Revelation 7:1–3, MEV

Once again, four angels are involved in the vision John is seeing, just like the four angelic creatures of the seals and the horsemen of the apocalypse. Seems to be a pattern here, doesn't it?

Now, there are many who believe that these winds, which are to cause harm across the world, are evil in nature, and why not? I am not saying they are wrong, but I get something different when reading about the angels "holding the four winds of the earth."

As my Bible reads, those responsible, or those "to whom it was granted to harm the earth and the sea," are angels (v. 2). This part of Scripture was written in Greek, and the verse uses the Greek word *angelos*,[2] which is the plural form of the same word previously used for the angel who is in possession of the seal of the living God. This angel is granted the authority to command the others to refrain from harming the earth until the angels have sealed the 144,000 of Israel, that is, of the nation of Israel, or those who are direct descendants of the twelve tribes, as it is so written by John (vv. 2–8).

These 144,000 are not Gentiles, because they cannot be Gentiles, according to the Word. They hail from the bloodline of Abraham and the other patriarchs. This remnant of Israel will be spared from certain persecutions and God's wrath upon the earth.

What John then sees with the multitude, the saints, and the church triumphant has not happened yet: "Behold, a great multitude which no one could number, of all nations, tribes, peoples, and tongues, standing before the throne and before the Lamb, clothed with white robes, with palm branches in their hands" (v. 9). This is the group he longs to be a part of when the time comes. As they wave the palm fronds to glorify the Lamb and the Father, how could he not remember the same event that happened when Jesus rode into Jerusalem on the colt of a donkey? (See John 12.)

John had seen this before, but now Jesus and the Father are given the praise they are worthy of on a scale that is cosmic and unable to be calculated. John now also listens to the saints celebrate and praise the Ones who gave them salvation from the sinful world that sought to separate them from their Creator. They have finally finished the race and no longer have to fight, for the Lamb and His army will take over the battle.

Next, the creatures of the throne and the elders all bow and worship the King when the saints praise God, much like when John witnessed the elders bow and cast their crowns before the throne when the creatures glorified God. Now there is a transference of authority to the saints, who were created in God's image.

But let's be clear: The saints are granted limited authority in Jesus Christ, not ultimate authority that rivals His. While we will rule with Him, we do not rule as Him.

John continues,

> One of the elders answered, saying to me, "Who are these arrayed in white robes, and where did they come from?"
> And I said to him, "Sir, you know."
> —REVELATION 7:13–14

As one of the elders poses what seems to me to be a rhetorical question, I find myself asking: Could this elder be the same one as before? He and John both know the elder is aware of who the saints that worship at the throne are, and John wisely shows respect and submission in his answer, hoping perhaps to learn the identity of the assembly of the saints.

Again, is this a prophet of old whom John addresses with such respect? Is John possibly viewing his own brother in a state of elevation and reward?

For the time being, we do not have the answer to these questions, but the Book of Revelation and the Bible as a whole hold within them wonders that we should ponder—without, of course, leaving the pages of doctrine for heretical ways of thought.

Asking questions is not a bad thing, but coming to unverified answers most certainly can be. I'm not sure about you, but I have a whole list of questions that, if given the opportunity, I plan on bringing before the Lord!

Regardless, the elder tells John that the saints have their new lives and bodies now, constantly in the presence of God and no longer thirsty or hungry, for Jesus will lead them to living waters, and there will be no more pain or hurt (vv. 14–17).

When you hear the lies of anti-Semites, like Nick Fuentes and the Islamic regime in Iran, talking about Israel in the same tone, you can rest assured these voices are not on the side of God. They stand firmly against Him, deceived by the devil yet so sure they are right.

CHAPTER 8

The SILENCE of HEAVEN

THE BREAKING OF the final seal. The beginning of the trumpets.

> When He opened the seventh seal, there was silence in heaven for about half an hour. And I saw the seven angels who stand before God, and seven trumpets were given to them.
> —REVELATION 8:1–2, MEV

John must be in a state of extreme apprehension during the silence following the breaking of that final seal. What cosmic-scale event is about to take place? The level of anticipation has to be palpable for John while heaven goes silent.

Meanwhile, seven angels are about to be granted extreme levels of authority.

How great is that authority granted to these seven who are about to usher in God's wrath with the blowing of the trumpets and the beginning of the end of the age?

The censer, the holder of the saints' prayers, is strange to think of this way, but this is an offering that is pleasing and accepted by the Lord in heaven.

> Then another angel, having a golden censer, came and stood at the altar. He was given much incense, that he should offer it with the prayers of all the saints.... And the smoke of the incense, with the prayers of the saints, ascended before God from the angel's hand. Then the angel took the censer, filled it with fire from the altar, and threw it to the earth. And there were noises, thunderings, lightnings, and an earthquake.
> —REVELATION 8:3–5

The Bible gives examples of offerings that are rejected by the Lord—take Cain, for example—yet according to the passage in Revelation, the aroma and smoke of the incense rise before God in His throne room, accepted before all heaven.

God would not allow an imperfect sacrifice to be performed in His throne room. Those imperfect sacrifices are of an earthly place, not the holiest place in existence. This act is the Lord fulfilling prophecy and keeping His word that vengeance is His and His alone, and it will be carried out.

The casting of the saints' prayers—often created through pain and tears but filled with faith and infused with God's holy, purifying fire—is in preparation for what is coming next with the blowing of the trumpets of judgment.

There is a cleansing purpose behind doing this. The Lord is taking these prayers, given up to Him in a fallen world, and correcting the wrongs that were committed against Him, because that is what sin is at its heart: an affront to God and His design, order, power, majesty, holiness, and righteousness. He cannot allow it in His presence; hence, Satan needed to be cast out of heaven.

One angel is chosen to cast God's judgment from His holy altar onto the earth; the other seven angels recognize this and ready themselves for the moment God has prepared them for.

I think back to the prayers and utterings of the saints from below the altar of God that John witnessed previously.

Could this pouring out of the fire of God upon the earth with the holy censer be a part of the reason the saints had to wait for the Lord's vengeance? If it is a part of the timeline of God's revenge for His saints, it is yet another marvelous example of God answering our prayers, but often not in the way or the time frame in which we think they should be answered.

But just as with all other aspects of God, His timing is perfect.

THE FIRST TRUMPET

Even as the trumpet sounds, delivering judgment upon the unrepentant earth, it also continues to serve as a warning for them.

> The first angel sounded....And a third of the trees were burned up, and all green grass was burned up.
> —REVELATION 8:7

Just as Pharaoh was given multiple opportunities to repent yet did not due to his hardened heart, so too is mercy shown by God during the trumpet judgments. But many will refuse it, just as Pharaoh did (Exod. 7–11).

This warning, and more to follow it, is for those enduring the judgment to repent and turn away from their wicked ways. But these warnings should not take away the severity of the judgment delivered by angels according to God's plan. We live in a wicked world, and "the wages of sin is death" (Rom. 6:23).

The striking of vegetation will impact more than just the food supply. The CO_2 that climate alarmists are always up in arms about (with their doomsday predictions always coming and going) will most likely go up. With fewer natural air purifiers the makeup of the earth's atmosphere will change. Many still will deny the Lord's hand in these events and claim them to be natural.

Of course, this assumes the events John witnesses are not symbolic but are, in fact, literal events that are to occur in the world as the current age draws to an end. I am in the camp that believes literal events will be occurring when the angels sound their trumpets, but spiritual events will likely be taking place on the earth as well.

In whatever manner this event takes place, just imagine the chaos and deception from humanity to try to cover this event up.

The media would go into a frenzy when such a catastrophic

event takes place. World leadership would try to figure out a way to spin this into a story that is not judgment from God, because as the devil roams the earth, he does not want the people in it repenting of their sins.

People will be looking, searching, and desperate for answers. There is the Bible, of course, that will tell them everything that is taking place and what is to come, but that is not what the leadership of the world will be telling them. No, it will be the opposite of that—more deception, more lies, more anti-God rhetoric.

THE SECOND TRUMPET

The imagery described by John as the angel blows the second trumpet suggests a meteor of some type that will strike the oceans, devastating marine life. But bear with me just a moment and consider the phrasing John uses, translated from the Greek as "as it were a great mountain" or "something like a great mountain" (KJV, NKJV).

> And something like a great mountain burning with fire was thrown into the sea, and a third of the sea became blood.
> —REVELATION 8:8

Mind you, John is describing something he possibly has no understanding of. Perhaps, and this is just a potential theory, it is some sort of large satellite, or even a space station.

John would not have the verbiage to explain the sight of such a construct falling into the ocean and potentially leaking some type of chemical, spreading mass contamination.

Again, this is nothing more than a possible theory of how the Lord may accomplish His biblical prophecy that will occur. But it's fun to think about and wonder how things are going to take shape during the end of the current age.

The Silence of Heaven

Whether the waters turn into literal or metaphorical blood, the wildlife in the world's oceans will suffer catastrophic losses. The international fishing economy will suffer with the loss of one-third of their product, which in turn will drive the prices for seafood higher, and who knows what inflation will look like at the time around the globe. (See Revelation 8:9.)

The devastation will be even worse than fish being removed from the ecosystem, however. Shrimp, coral reefs, sharks, whales, crabs, lobsters, you name it—if it is in the ocean, according to John in the literal interpretation, one-third will be gone (v. 9).

Now, when you look at the "as it were" or "something like" a mountain being thrown into the ocean, ask if this could lead to a catastrophic tsunami.

In my lifetime we've seen such destruction in the Indian Ocean,[1] described as one of the largest natural disasters in recorded history, killing approximately 228,000 people as it struck about a dozen different countries. It left behind in its wake billions in damages, an unknown number of people missing, and regions devastated at the loss of farming, business, and housing.

Yet this pales in comparison to what a truly apocalyptic tsunami brought upon by God's vengeance would bring, especially a tsunami that would see one-third of the earth's ocean vessels destroyed, as John describes (v. 9).

How will the loss of a third of the world's ships impact trade? How much will countries and businesses lose in products and personnel?

Should a third of the ships sink into the ocean, that in and of itself would create a massive ecological disaster with chemicals poisoning the waters they sink in, perhaps on a scale unmanageable for humanity.

The interconnectedness that nature and humanity share is often overlooked in our hyperconsumerist societies of today.

Many people take for granted the bounties of the ocean the Lord has blessed us with, and this will be revealed when God takes away a part of it.

Economies will collapse from this shake-up, entire industries will go bankrupt, and lives will be permanently upended by the devastation.

THE THIRD TRUMPET

With the third trumpet, we hear of the great star named Wormwood (v. 11). Many believers have at least heard this name, even if in passing.

John describes this catastrophic event as "a great star [falling] from heaven" (v. 10). Like the second trumpet, I cannot help but wonder if this is a literal star, perhaps sent by the Lord's hand; an asteroid or meteor, like the movies depict hitting earth; or possibly a creation of man's own hand.

For now I lean toward a natural body that would fall from the heavens, but should any country launch a satellite, space station, or spaceship in my lifetime named Wormwood, you best believe I'm paying attention to that!

While the second trumpet affected the oceans and salted bodies of water, this trumpet may bring with it a far harsher penalty: the loss of large swathes of drinkable fresh water.

The blowing of the third trumpet is only two verses long but brings unimaginable difficulty in those two verses: "The third angel sounded: And a great star fell from heaven, burning like a torch, and it fell on a third of the rivers and on the springs of water....A third of the waters became wormwood, and many men died from the water, because it was made bitter" (vv. 10–11).

A glaring question arises from these verses: Where will Wormwood hit that will poison so much water and bring about so much death?

In trying to plot a potential location, all which is purely

speculation of course, will this star impact a singular location, or will it break up into multiple pieces, striking multiple places on earth?

Think of some of the largest bodies of fresh water, as well as the largest river basins, in the world. There are the Great Lakes, Lake Victoria, the Amazon River basin, the Congo and Nile River basins in Africa—all are gigantic purveyors of fresh water.

But which one would lead to *many men* dying from the Wormwood poisoning?

The Danube and Rhine Rivers would likely poison as many people as (if not far more than) the entire Amazon basin due to population density, while the Mississippi River and its tributaries being poisoned would spell doom for the United States. Meanwhile, it is estimated that some 400 million plus people rely on the Yangtze River in China, or approximately one-third of the country's population.[2]

Regardless of where the poisoning takes place, it will be catastrophic, but in different ways than the oceans being struck.

Trade will be hit much harder during the second trumpet, but socially, the third trumpet may hit harder. With fresh water being the target, people will grow thirsty, leading to the loss of life John writes about. Farming will be hugely impacted, leading to famines and more loss of life. More businesses will shut down.

One thing I did not mention in the second-trumpet section is this: When trade is impacted and businesses and banks shut down from the impact of the judgments placed on the earth, who will step in to seize control? My money is on whatever forms of government are in place at the time—perhaps even a one-world government.

World leaders and globalists would be more than happy to swoop in and seize as much economic, social, and political power as they could as countries reel from these events.

THE FOURTH TRUMPET

All the while the people of the world will be looking for answers to their problems, or a savior, paving the way for the Antichrist to assert control.

I sometimes feel we live in a time when we doubt God's ability, or perhaps willingness, to interact with the physical, natural world. But what folly it is to think such a thing. The Word of God is replete with examples of God answering prayers offered in faith and in accordance with His will and command.

When reading the text in a literal sense, I cannot help but think of what God did in answer to Joshua's prayer:

> So the sun stood still, and the moon stood in place until the people brought vengeance on their enemies. Is this not written in the book of Jashar? The sun stood still in the middle of the sky and did not set for about a full day. There has not been a day like this either before or after it, when the Lord obeyed a man, for the Lord waged war for Israel.
> —Joshua 10:13–14, MEV

If the trumpets are meant as a continuation and part of the final judgment of God, it makes perfect sense that the natural world is in its death throes.

> The fourth angel sounded: And a third of the sun was struck, a third of the moon, and a third of the stars, so that a third of them were darkened. A third of the day did not shine, and likewise the night.
> —Revelation 8:12

When sin entered the physical realm, all existence was contaminated, not just the earth. The sun, the moon, the stars—all will be subject to God's judgment of the current age, as will be the case when a third of each celestial body will grow dark.

With the blowing of every trumpet up to this point—never mind the seals that were broken prior—the farming and agriculture on earth is going to be left utterly devastated.

Mass famine, mass starvation, mass economic upheaval, mass migration to where there is available food and water, mass social control, and restraints in the wake of this devastation—this is not a world I hope to be in when these judgments are carried out!

A celestial event of such magnitude could manifest in many ways, or perhaps the sun, moon, and a third of the stars simply begin shutting down by the command of God. Who is to say?

CHAPTER 9

DEMON LOCUSTS and ANGELS

So far the trumpets have been directed only at the earth, and of course, they indirectly affect humanity and all living creatures on the planet. Then, with the massive blackout and the chaos that ensues, the three woes (the next three trumpets) are released upon the earth by the eagle-like angel that declares their impending arrival.

The biblical text often points to this angelic messenger as an eagle; some, from what I've seen, have also made the interpretation of a vulture. Whichever form this angel has, the message remains the same: The inhabitants of the earth are about to experience a very painful and distressing time due to the next three trumpets sounding.

The Fifth Trumpet

Now John witnesses the beginning of the three woes being brought against the unrepentant of the earth. A storm of spiritual warfare is unleashed upon the earth, so great it must be announced throughout the heavens.

John witnesses what is presumed to be a fallen angel (perhaps even a demon or Satan himself, but this is not the place to debate whether a fallen angel is a demon, or vice versa, and the differences between the two) given power to release a horde of demonic entities upon the earth (Rev. 9:1–3).

John's spiritual maturity does not show fear at the sight of this trumpet sounding, for he knows even he has power over the fallen spirit because of the power of the Holy Spirit that

Demon Locusts and Angels

lives in him. This fallen being can only do what the Lord allows it to do: unleash judgment from the pit onto the unredeemed.

> And he opened the bottomless pit, and smoke arose out of the pit....Then out of the smoke locusts came upon the earth. And to them was given power....They were commanded not to harm the grass of the earth, or any green thing, or any tree, but only those men who do not have the seal of God on their foreheads. And they were not given authority to kill them, but to torment them for five months....
>
> ...And they had as king over them the angel of the bottomless pit, whose name in Hebrew is Abaddon, but in Greek he has the name Apollyon.
> —Revelation 9:2–5, 11

Even the locusts, be they creations of God specifically for this event or demons set apart to obey God's command, fall into obedience to the Lord's boundaries for them.

This is yet another example of the many times God has given something or someone authority to bring about judgment to those who were warned yet did not repent. (See the two times the nation of Israel, God's chosen people, was destroyed.)

Abaddon's (Apollyon's) army will travel the earth during these five months.

I am of the belief that these creatures are not literal, as are many others. This is simply my view as well: The earth will not see a stampede of these creatures because they will be released from a spiritual prison, not a physical one.

When they are released, unimaginable torment will fill the earth. The natural realm—the grass, the trees, and any green thing—as well as the people marked by God will be exempt from this torment.

The destroyer will bring about immense suffering upon all those not protected by the mark of God: societies, cultures, economies, armies, families, and false churches. All these will structurally crumble under his march, but they will not die by his hand—just as God limited Satan from killing His servant Job.

What is absolutely crazy when you read these verses about Abaddon (did you know he also holds a place in society? I'll mention this in a moment) is he is specifically listed as *king* over these demonic forces, but he is an angel.

If you were even aware of Abaddon, did you think he was a demon? I did for a very long time.

But that is why knowing the Word of God is so important! This is not some made-up, imaginary character; this is a real-life ruler of darkness! And I hold Abaddon in that level of hierarchy over Satan's forces. He is a king of demons, and a very real one at that.

We live in a day and age when demons, principalities, powers, and rulers of darkness are given a place in society as characters in media, video games, literature, and just about every realm of culture.

This includes Abaddon.

It is extremely easy to find examples of Lucifer, the Antichrist, and the evil spirit Lilith, but with Abaddon not nearly as many people are aware of his sizable influence.

There is a science fiction "universe" that has drawn millions into reading its books, collecting and building its miniatures, and playing its video games. Soon, there will even be a TV series based on it, and the demons that inhabit this series, known as *Warhammer*.

One of the many antagonists in the series is Abaddon the Despoiler,[1] and many a youth have been drawn into this action-packed universe filled with demons and the worship of a god-emperor.

What realm of media has Satan not infected with the

desensitization of demonic entities, even to the point where demons are the good guys?

It is all planned and purposeful, to draw people away from the truth found within the Word of God to join Lucifer and his minions in the lake of fire for all eternity.

THE SIXTH TRUMPET

John continues,

> I heard a voice from the four horns of the golden altar which is before God…"Release the four angels who are bound at the great Euphrates River." And the four angels…were released to kill one-third of mankind.
> —REVELATION 9:13–15, MEV

Whenever the topic of the angels in place on the Euphrates River (in modern-day Iraq) arises, I find myself wondering: Are these in some way affiliated with, or perhaps even are they, the angels set in place to protect the Garden of Eden? Is there still a physical manifestation of the garden here on earth?

Regardless, the voice that comes forth from the altar—the same altar where the angel filled the censer with incense due to the cries of the saints—commands the angels to kill one-third of mankind.

One. Third.

Reading from the pages of the Word of God, I feel like we sometimes lose sight of just how monumental the events that take place within the Bible truly are. Billions are set to be killed from the forces unleashed by the angels of the Euphrates.

The world was set ablaze when 1,200 Israelis were brutally massacred by the terrorist organization Hamas on October 7, 2023. Can anyone imagine what the aftermath would be like in a world where literal billions will die at once?

This time described in the Bible strikes me as a period of great warfare and unrest across the globe.

Amid these events that reveal a lack of peace on earth, John specifically mentions a force of two hundred million—whether it be a spiritual or a literal army—that will wreak havoc upon the earth.

> Now the number of the army of the horsemen was two hundred million....I saw the horses in the vision: those who sat on them had breastplates of fiery red, hyacinth blue, and sulfur yellow; and the heads of the horses were like the heads of lions; and out of their mouths came fire, smoke, and brimstone. By these three plagues a third of mankind was killed—by the fire and the smoke and the brimstone.
> —REVELATION 9:16–17

Just think about all John has witnessed up to this point.

Was this a draining event for John as he witnessed untold destruction and perhaps things or devices he could not fully comprehend due to the massive technological difference between his day and the modern era? Or was John given spiritual insight into what modernity looks like and fully understood and grasped every aspect of what he saw as he wrote it down for future generations to read?

What do the horsemen John describes sound like to you? I personally can see how they could be interpreted as a literal army. Specifically, as they spit fire, smoke, and brimstone from their mouths, a column of tanks comes to mind.

Tank warfare is especially effective in the Middle East (remember the Persian Gulf War?), where Iran resides—one of the greatest threats to Israel.

Throughout the years, the US has effectively used tank warfare in the region, while Israel also has a large tank force to protect its homeland.

But what other ways could fire, smoke, and brimstone kill a third of humanity?

Wildfires also come to mind and have proven to be extremely difficult for humans to bring under control. Smoke is a by-product of such an event, poisoning the air and making it difficult, if not impossible, to breathe in such a situation.

But that still leaves brimstone, also known by a more common term: sulfur. Well, what are some of the purposes sulfur is commonly used for?

A short list of uses includes making fertilizer, water processing, oil refining, mineral extraction, and making car batteries.[2]

But there is one other way sulfur has been used for decades, and it's deadly.

Sulfur is one of the main components in sulfur dioxide (SO_2), which is one of the most used materials in chemical warfare, going back millennia.

Could this deadly chemical concoction be a part of the third plague brought upon mankind once the angels of the Euphrates are unleashed and their army of two hundred million horsemen is unleashed upon the world?

As the angels are released, terror is going to be released with them. Yet John and the Holy Spirit find it important enough to ensure the number *two hundred million* is recorded in His Word, pointing to the massive spiritual warfare that will be taking place during this time.

The Lord did not see fit to entrust the slaying of billions to the fallen angel Abaddon; instead, this duty falls upon His chosen warriors. Evil cannot cast out evil, and in this purge of the unrepentant, billions will die while billions more continue to refuse repentance.

Even as the world descends rapidly toward the Lord's final judgments, the hearts of many will remain cold. John describes them as refusing, being stubborn and hard-hearted to some of the final warnings from their Creator (v. 20).

What stands out most profoundly to me now, in the days we are currently living in, is John's pointing out that they worship demons and idols (v. 20).

All around the world in today's age demonic worship is erupting at an advanced pace. Working in Christian media, I see it almost daily, and it isn't even hidden anymore! People absolutely refuse to acknowledge the spiritual warfare that is taking place in the world and give these demonic entities free reign over a multitude of fronts in society: government, media, even the church.

Television showcases demonic entities as the protagonists, mocking God's values, morals, and righteousness; idols are set up as statues in major cities; money and self are worshipped above God. Yes, the world has already made the turn into demonism and is only sinking deeper and deeper into it.

And what exactly are the three areas of sin so egregious, so ingrained in an unrepentant world, that God saw fit to have His servant John include them in the final book of the Bible?

1. Murder

This act, begun by Cain in the very first generation of life after Adam and Eve (Gen. 4), continues until the end of days. The lack of appreciation and respect for life enables people to commit such heinous crimes, as does a lack of respect for authority or of any whim of personal responsibility.

We are seeing this mentality, this spirit, of lawlessness across the world as crimes are going unpunished and unprosecuted, emboldening further and more heinous crimes to take place in society.

2. Sorceries

At Charisma Media, where I serve as a staff writer and copy editor, we get mocked—quite often, in fact—for writing articles calling out the occult practices within the world as we see them. Many times witchcraft (a form of sorcery) is performed by the very idols, aka celebrities, that young people look to as sources of entertainment. Meanwhile, their parents are none the wiser.

Don't believe me? Take the biggest name in the world of entertainment today: Taylor Swift. A perfect example of the occult and New Age embedded in much of her music is the song "Karma." I will certainly not repeat all the lyrics of that song, as it takes the Lord's name in vain multiple times (which should be a red flag for any Christian). She refers to *karma* as a god and her boyfriend and uses idolatrous imagery throughout the entire music video. It has been viewed by millions upon millions of her fans, desensitizing them to the occult in the process.

Frankly, it is quite easy to see how the world will delve further into the occult to the point where they will not repent of it before God, because that would mean giving up the celebrities and idols that have opened them up to sorcery. This is because they become enveloped in spiritual chains by immersing themselves in such practices, and demons do not easily give up their prizes. Spiritual warfare is not just an important part of the Christian walk; it is essential to break these spiritual holds that have taken up residence in people's lives and seek to drag them down the path of eternal torment, separate from their Creator.

3. Sexual Immorality

This could be a book in and of itself. Where do I even begin?

The dominant societies of this world have all but abandoned God's design for sexuality. We as humans have come up with nearly every avenue possible to avoid the repercussions of intercourse, which ends up creating new life.

Countries around the globe have bent their knees before the

flag of "pride" and rejected a singular, heterosexual relationship as the design for humanity.

In many ways, the traditional marriage and family are routinely under attack by those who are, many times, unaware they are simply pawns of the devil to tear down that which God established.

We are living in a day when the next sexual revolution is not just being planned anymore but is well underway: the campaign to legalize and accept pedophilia in society.

Don't act shocked—many politicians within the United States are already pushing for this and call pedophiles by a new nomenclature: Minor Attracted Persons, or MAPs.

The transgender revolution already went off, and while there are those who are pushing back and fighting against this false ideology, it has been firmly implanted in many aspects of society and is still being crammed down every facet of culture it can be.

Lawmakers in California are already weakening the penalties for those who are caught in disgusting acts with minors,[3] and as has become the norm, they are looking to implement the state's demented laws on the rest of the nation.

It truly sickens me to see what the state that I was born in has become. Not a modern-day Sodom and Gomorrah, but worse.

Not only do I firmly believe these acts are going to be pushed through like the biologically impossible gender ideologies, but as time goes on, people will fight to be able to engage in such perverse acts.

John states people will refuse to repent of sexual depravity and instead cling to this lifestyle that leads to sickness and death (Rev. 9:21). And that is why more judgment awaits them. As John highlights the sins humans refuse to give up, he also highlights the strength spiritual bondage can have over a person's life.

This is what Christians go up against when they engage in

spiritual warfare, and it is clear that many believers are not properly equipped or discipled enough to go against such forces.

Along with John's list, Paul's writings and the Law given to Moses point to sexual sins and immorality as a cause for the Lord's severe judgment (as well as a major cause for the flood).

What is meant to be an act of intimacy between a man and a woman that is reflective of the intimacy between Christ and His church is instead corrupted and twisted to please the unnatural urges and burnings of the flesh.

Included in these judgments of the time will be the apostate church—the church that makes false claims about the sins that are grieving the Lord's heart.

CHAPTER 10

The MIGHTY ANGEL

You have to give John credit for his amazing level of discernment for heavenly beings.

> I saw still another mighty angel coming down from heaven, clothed with a cloud. And a rainbow was on his head, his face was like the sun, and his feet like pillars of fire. He had a little book open in his hand. And he set his right foot on the sea and his left foot on the land.
> —Revelation 10:1–2

John has enough knowledge, wisdom, presence of mind, and spiritual maturity to know the angel is mighty. Still below the Son, of course, but it strikes me as the spiritual equivalent to David's "mighty men" (2 Sam. 23) and the power and authority (along with submission to their leader) that they wielded.

Not a messenger angel like Gabriel, but a warrior.

This mighty angel is elevated high enough by God to be given a crown, and not just any crown but a rainbow, the symbol of God's promise, which always rings true and is present in His throne room.

The seven voices of thunder John hears are quite clearly the voice of God (Rev. 10:3–4); Scripture verifies in multiple places that the voice of God thunders. But when I read this, I wonder, since the Father, Son, and Holy Spirit are Three in One and One in Three, could these seven specific thunders be the voices of the Spirits of God as mentioned in Scripture? Previous references do not refer to God the Father in plural form, but they do with the Spirit of God. Perhaps I am splitting hairs here, but that is the amazing thing about the Book of Revelation: It really makes you think and wonder.

These seven thunders prophesy to John, but then the voice of the Father issues instructions to John not to write down what they say. Much like the Holy Spirit reveals to us the will of God, as the helper Jesus promised who is alive and well on the earth today, so too do the spirits reveal a mystery of God to John.

But it is not time for this particular revelation to be made known, and that drives an inquisitive person like me absolutely crazy. What it is time for is for John to witness a truly incredible sight.

He bears witness to a mighty angel taking an oath before the God of creation, something I am quite sure the angelic being took extremely seriously, that the delay of final judgment is over. It is time for the harshest of judgments upon the earth before the return of the King of kings, who is coming with a sword and bringing war with Him.

The angel tells John to eat the little book.

> I took the little book out of the angel's hand and ate it, and it was as sweet as honey in my mouth. But when I had eaten it, my stomach became bitter. And he said to me, "You must prophesy again about many peoples, nations, tongues, and kings."
> —REVELATION 10:10–11

Bear with me on this next part—it is totally theoretical and made of things that I wonder whenever I read through Revelation.

With John's consumption of the book and his task to still prophesy to the nations, will he play a part in the end of days, or was his task fulfilled within his life?

Which brings me to another branch of that theory: If John is to testify during the end of days, is John possibly still alive in some sort of stasis or perhaps hidden by the Lord somewhere on the earth, much like the angels of the Euphrates?

Trust me, I know this sounds crazy, but since there are so many conflicting reports about John's death and no concrete information—regardless of what the church in Ephesus says (I am of the mind his grave is not there)—what if the Lord has hidden him away for another time?

For centuries the most widely accepted view has been that John spent his final years in Ephesus, where he ministered and eventually died. The Basilica of St. John, built in the sixth century by the Byzantine emperor Justinian, stands as a monument to this belief, covering what many have claimed to be John's tomb.[1] Early Christian writers like Irenaeus (second century) and Eusebius (fourth century) attest to John's presence in Ephesus, though they stop short of explicitly confirming his burial there.[2] Yet despite the centuries of veneration, there's a major problem—no bodily remains have ever been found. Unlike the apostles Peter and Paul, whose supposed relics are enshrined in Rome, John's physical presence is missing. This lack of evidence has fueled various alternative theories.

One of the most intriguing ideas is that John never actually died.[3] This notion stems from a conversation recorded in John 21:22–23 where Jesus tells Peter, "If I want him to remain until I come, what is that to you?" (NASB). Some early Christians interpreted this to mean John had been taken up to heaven, like Elijah or Enoch, and thus never needed a burial site at all. While this theory isn't widely held in scholarly circles today, it persisted enough through history to add to the mystery.

Then, there's the theory that John was buried elsewhere. Some speculate he may have been buried on the island of Patmos, where he wrote the Book of Revelation while exiled. But no historical records or archaeological findings support this claim. Others suggest that John returned to Jerusalem in his final years and was buried there. Again, there's little to verify this idea, making it more of a pious legend than a grounded historical claim.

So where does that leave us? If John was buried in Ephesus, why is there no physical evidence? If he wasn't buried there, why did early Christians believe he was? And if he truly was taken up into heaven, why did later traditions develop around a supposed tomb? These are the kinds of lingering questions that make the study of biblical history so fascinating.

Again, that is the point of this book: to talk about the Book of Revelation! To discuss it with one another and to dig deep into Scripture.

Perhaps the utterings of the seven thunders are instructions to John regarding the Lord's mission for him. We, of course, cannot know this for certain; anyone who says otherwise is deceiving you. But I love theorizing and thinking about possibilities while ensuring I do not force thoughts and ideas into Scripture.

We should ponder and meditate on the Word but never add our own thoughts to it.

Reading Revelation throughout my life has always stirred a great desire in me to travel to the island of Patmos and look around at the places John was known to have inhabited.

Of course, much of the island has been excavated, and I am far from the first person to think of this, but I can never shake the idea that maybe, in the most minute of maybes, the disciple John is alive somewhere.

It is more doubtful than not. But I am not one to trod on an imagination, as long as that imagination is controlled.

CHAPTER 11

The TWO WITNESSES

THERE IS, OF course, spiritual insight to John's instruction to measure the temple (the temple that is still being debated today), and as with the trumpets, there are physical implications as well.

> I was given a reed like a measuring rod. And the angel stood, saying, "Rise and measure the temple of God, the altar, and those who worship there. But leave out the court which is outside the temple, and do not measure it, for it has been given to the Gentiles. And they will tread the holy city underfoot for forty-two months."
>
> —REVELATION 11:1–2

The temple, I wholeheartedly believe, will be built a third time, and sacrifices will take place within its grounds again. *The court* may very well be the courtyard defiled on the Temple Mount by the Dome of the Rock.[1]

Like with Moses and the burning bush, this ground where God has dwelled in the past is holy.

Preparations are already well underway through groups such as the Temple Institute to furnish a rebuilt temple in Jerusalem, including the prophetic red heifers.[2]

Looking at the Temple Mount these days, you wonder just how God is going to pull off such an amazing feat, since the grounds are currently being usurped by the Dome of the Rock and the Al-Aqsa Mosque.

For those who have been paying attention since the massacre committed by the terror organization Hamas on

October 7, 2023, however, we've seen how quickly antisemitism has spread around the world.

So if the whole world is against Israel, what would there be to stop Israel from retaking their Temple Mount from a false god? I know that sounds harsh, but the reality is God's will is going to be done, one way or the other.

The angel continues telling John,

> And I will give power to my two witnesses, and they will prophesy for one thousand two hundred and sixty days, clothed in sackcloth.
> —REVELATION 11:3, MEV

The two witnesses are, of course, witnesses (ha ha) to God and the Messiah, yet the angel tells John they are his! How often have we overlooked this little bit in the chain of command in heaven?

My take on this is they are certainly servants of the Most High God, but they are under the authority of this particular angel while their mission is underway.

This mission, of course, lasts for 1,260 days (about three and a half years, or forty-two months). During this time, the two witnesses have the power and authority to bring plagues upon their adversaries should they so choose (vv. 5–6).

Now, what always caught my attention, especially when I was a youth, was that they have built-in flamethrowers in their mouths!

Perhaps this is metaphorical, meaning they have some of the best sermons in the history of the world lined up for those who will hear their words, or they will breathe literal fire and terrify a world that is enclosed in darkness when it tries to lay its hands on them.

And now, ladies and gentlemen, we arrive at the often-discussed theory that no one will ever be able to prove until the time the Lord allows it to be revealed: Just who are these two witnesses?

Well, my dear reader, I certainly have my theory on the two, and many others have theirs, as well as those who hold the same thoughts as my own.

I firmly stand in the camp that believes the two witnesses are the only two men not to taste death, according to the Bible. And remember, even Jesus tasted death (He, however, overcame it). That would be Enoch and Elijah.

Should you be in the group that believes these are, in fact, spiritual witnesses, meaning the church are the ones witnessing and being persecuted against, that is fine. This is not a salvational issue, simply a difference of interpretation of scriptures and what the mysteries in the Book of Revelation mean.

These things need to be discussed among the faithful. Christians need to be able to defend their positions from a biblical standpoint and truly understand the who, what, where, when, and why behind their beliefs.

For far too long we have been an ankle-deep church. It is time to put our total and complete faith in the Lord and jump into the deep end with both feet and become, as Paul called himself, "fools for Christ" (1 Cor. 4:10, AMP).

We must know our history and where we came from. We must know the *why* behind our faith so that we can tell others about Him. If we cannot explain the life, death, burial, and resurrection of Jesus to those who do not believe, then what are we doing?

Open, clear, respectful dialogue helps prepare the church for discussing such topics with those who are curious about Jesus and who He truly is, as well as those who are hostile to the gospel message.

Again, I am not definitively stating the two witnesses are

The Two Witnesses

Enoch and Elijah; no one can do that in truth. But this is what I feel is most logical according to the laws of God.

They were both whisked into heaven by the Lord for a reason. It was not an arbitrary whisking away. Everything God does has purpose, and that is evidenced throughout His Word.

For every human to taste death it would mean that at some point Elijah and Enoch must drink from that cup as well, and according to the inerrant Scriptures, the two witnesses will be killed: "When they have finished their testimony, the beast that ascends from the bottomless pit will wage war against them...and kill them. Their dead bodies will lie in the street of the great city...where also our Lord was crucified." (Rev. 11:7–8, MEV).

Moses is another strong contender who many believe will join Elijah as one of the two witnesses, but I simply do not see how that could be, as the Bible clearly states Moses died and was buried (Deut. 34). How then could Moses suffer a second death?

The Bible has multiple examples of resurrections taking place aside from Jesus' (Lazarus, anyone?) and of the resurrected then going on to lead fulfilled lives, but not of resurrections taking place after millennia have passed and the physical body has decayed and eroded. They always came back to the original bodies they were born in.

Many think Moses may be one of the two witnesses due to their ability, while on earth, to bring about plagues upon the remnants of humanity who stand against them. I personally do not buy into this, for while it was Moses and Aaron who were used to bring the plagues upon Egypt, it was by God's power that this happened. They were the delivery vessels, not the power supplies.

Now, there are lines of thought that do not believe these verses regarding the two witnesses refer to Jerusalem proper or the literal location of the city but instead believe they take place in a world filled with evil.

For me this is a matter that needs prayer and discernment on every believer's part when they read the scriptures. I believe these events will take place in Israel, where Jesus was crucified. Part of this reasoning is the central position that Israel holds when it comes to biblical end-times prophecy.

Allow me to spell straight out for you where I stand: I am completely and 100 percent against replacement theology, where the Christian church completely takes the place of national Israel. This is a dangerous and unbiblical notion that is not found anywhere in the Scriptures but is, in fact, proved false by them.

Take a step back from looking at Israel from a biblical lens, and look at it from a historical standpoint, and you will (or at least should) see that much of what has happened in regard to the Jewish people would be nearly impossible to accomplish without the Lord's hand at work.

The resurrection of the state of Israel in 1948 is positive proof of something that by the secular mind should never have happened, except it did because the Abrahamic covenant the Lord established back in the Book of Genesis is still very much in effect!

Jesus is the fulfillment of prophecy. He is the Messiah! He is the fulfillment of the Law (which He held in high regard, but that is another conversation for another day). Jesus loves His people, the Jews. This is evident throughout the Gospels.

It pains me to see so many who call themselves Christians in this day and age (although many are clearly not by their actions and words) hold antisemitic views against God's people. According to Scripture, if you hold this type of view and curse Israel, then you are literally inviting the Lord God to curse you for cursing His people (Gen. 12). It really is simple. Jesus came and fulfilled the Mosaic covenant (the Law), but He never says He is the fulfillment of the Abrahamic covenant (God's promise to Abram).

As Christians we have been invited into the fold of salvation with Israel. Jesus bridged that gap into the Lord's presence through His precious blood as the perfect and sinless sacrifice. Again, He is the fulfillment of the Law, but this is a separate unification from the Abrahamic covenant.

This is also why there will be war between the descendants of Ishmael and those of Isaac.

This is why there will never be true peace in the Middle East until the return of Jesus Christ, because of the word of the Lord in Genesis 16:12. Yes, the Bible says Isaac and Ishmael buried their father, Abraham, but this does not mean that they were reconciled, as some believe. The current state of the Middle East, especially when it comes to Israel, strongly showcases that the words spoken over Ishmael and his descendants are very much in play today.

THE WORLD OF THE BEAST

We can see today, in societies around the world, that the Word of God is becoming despised by many. The hatred the world has toward Jesus and His disciples is in full view today, and we are not nearly as far into the end-times as this period of the two witnesses.

They will preach, and the gospel will be told, and that hatred will swell to levels we simply do not see in modern society, but we are well on our way there. In this world—one I pray I am no longer a part of—the beast will be released from the same bottomless pit as the locusts, he will kill the two witnesses in full view of the world, and the world will rejoice (Rev. 11:7, 9–10).

John witnesses this, not knowing that modern-day media will allow for the whole world to see the bodies of the witnesses. When I read these verses in which their bodies will be on display for the whole world to see and celebrate their deaths, I think of the movie *Black Hawk Down*, which replicates the American soldier dragged through the streets of Mogadishu, Somalia.

Imagine broadcasts of their murdered bodies being shown and the earth rejoicing. YouTube videos being made to dispute the supernatural nature of these two men. TikTok videos cursing their names. Newscasts deceiving the public about their miracles and how this was not an act of God, according to the world.

Except in this case, a holiday appears to be established to commemorate the deaths of these men of God. The people will be merry and exchange gifts because the witnesses' convicting message will be silenced—for a short time.

> After the three and a half days, the breath of life from God entered them, and they stood on their feet, and great fear fell on those who saw them....And they ascended to heaven in a cloud.
> —Revelation 11:11, mev

After some time—perhaps a literal three and a half days, or perhaps this time frame just means after a period of time—God will resurrect these witnesses, and they will ascend into heaven for all the world to see.

Can you imagine the level of censorship in that day and age compared to today's budding censorship machine? The level of spin that earthly leaders will try to perform will be outrageous, perhaps even downright blacking out the event when people see what is happening.

But the truth always finds a way to get out.

Social media platforms will be on overdrive trying to censor various posts showing citizen videos of the ascension and the booming voice—presumably of God, but it could also be an angelic being who has been granted great authority by God—calling the witnesses into heaven.

The Two Witnesses

Perhaps this will be the second time for the witnesses to ascend into heaven. Regardless, they will taste death after completing the mission they are sent to earth for.

In all this darkness, in all this sin, God is still giving chance after chance for people to accept the salvation for which Jesus died and rose again.

As these witnesses ascend, their departure is marked by more earthly signs with heavenly perspectives. The earth will shake, and the city in which this is taking place will leave thousands dead, if you are viewing this from a literal standpoint.

But amid all this tragedy, a worldwide scale of terror and righteous judgment, there are those who finally cry out to God and glorify Him (v. 13). When this praise ascends to heaven and presents itself before the Lord, this marks the end of the second woe, with one more to go: the seventh trumpet.

As the sixth trumpet marks the end of a season, the seventh marks the beginning of the next. Its sounding throws heaven into uproarious praise, with the twenty-four elders yet again showering the Lord with worship.

Then, as the God of heaven is accepting His praise, which He is worthy of, God reveals His temple in heaven and a restored ark of the covenant.

No one knows what actually happened to the ark here on earth, but there sure are a lot of theories. I'm not going to dive into those because, really, it serves no purpose in furthering the kingdom of God. Could the ark be under the Temple Mount? Possibly, but one thing is certain: With or without the ark of the covenant, biblical prophecy will continue to be fulfilled, and Jesus Christ will return as the triumphant King.

While John is witnessing the ark in a spiritual vision, it shows him—and probably provides some amount of comfort to him, as a Messianic Jew—that God has not abandoned His people, and His great faithfulness will be with them until the end of time.

CHAPTER 12

JOHN'S VISION of the WOMAN

Now John moves on from receiving visions of the eventual judgments God has planned for the earth in its final hour to a series of visions that explain the spiritual warfare taking place from the very beginning.

From my perspective—and feel free to disagree (I am sure many will)—the woman John sees in this new vision is very much the nation of Israel.

Clothed in God's glory, represented by the sun, and adorned with a garland of twelve stars representing the twelve tribes, the woman in Revelation 12 stands upon the moon—a celestial body divinely placed as a firmament for Israel (v. 1). This imagery signifies Israel's foundational connection to the lunar cycle, which governs their calendar. Unlike the solar-based calendars of many nations, Israel's timekeeping follows the phases of the moon, a design ordained by God. Throughout history this lunar-based system has aligned with prophetic events, demonstrating its significance in God's timeline and reinforcing the role of Israel in biblical prophecy.

> And the dragon stood before the woman who was ready to give birth, to devour her Child as soon as it was born. She bore a male Child who was to rule all nations with a rod of iron.
> —Revelation 12:4–5

Through the nation of Israel, God sends the world salvation through Jesus Christ.

Waiting for Him is that vile enemy of God, Satan, represented by the dragon. Here is the description of the features of the dragon and what they mean, as listed in my *New Spirit-Filled Life Bible*:

> **Seven heads** represent complete authority, intelligence, and cleverness, but not wisdom (see Prov. 1:7). **Ten** represents earthly completeness, which is therefore limited. **Horns** are a symbol of physical or political strength. **Seven diadems** represent political authority.[1]

John has personally witnessed part of the signs detailed in this heavenly vision.

He knew, followed, and loved the child the woman birthed, who is Christ. John had given his life for the child, following the Messiah's example. He watched as Christ ascended to heaven after overcoming death and was caught up by God. He had cast out demons in the name of Jesus, but now he witnesses the fall of those angels and the one who deceived them: the dragon, who is Satan.

John also witnesses firsthand the anger, hate, and rage that drives Satan to steal, kill, destroy, and deceive everything and everyone he comes across. Satan's hatred is not meant to be underestimated, and John gives a warning respecting the power behind this adversary: He is great in power and fiery in manner.

The devil's ability to deceive and destroy should not in any way, shape, or form be taken lightly by the church. Yet all too many reduce him to a caricature of the powerful enemy he truly is.

John continues,

> And war broke out in heaven: Michael and his angels fought with the dragon; and the dragon and his angels fought, but they did not prevail, nor was a place found for them in heaven any longer.
> —REVELATION 12:7–8

His anger and hatred against God, who saw him removed from his station, are so great that there is nothing he will not do against the Lord's creation. Having knowledge of his own defeat and eventual demise, Satan still strikes out at heaven, knowing he cannot overcome Michael. But he is relentless to a point humans do not understand.

Satan works to kill the most innocent, mutilate and deform children, and break up and corrupt marriages that are representative of Jesus and His church. He makes war against the peaceful and torments the vulnerable and weak. Nothing is too far, too grotesque, too immoral, or too heinous for him to commit, all due to his hatred of God and His design, His power.

The only way Satan will be stopped is when he is locked up or destroyed in the lake of fire for eternity. This is why he wars so aggressively against the woman's offspring, the Root of Jesse, the Son of Man, the last Adam. For as long as the dragon has reign on the earth, neither Israel nor Christ's church will know peace, but they will instead be persecuted and harassed by the dragon and his minions (v. 17).

This is the spiritual warfare we are up against and why it is so important for believers to engage in it. In a time when we need to be interceding, warring, fasting, and taking the fight to the devil, people are instead losing faith and belief in the supernatural.

If this were not true, our society in America would not be transforming into the satanic, demonic, pagan, immoral, lawless shell of a formerly great nation.

But there is always hope!

Just as Michael and his angels defeated the dragon and witnessed him cast out of heaven, so do we have power over the enemy as well!

And that victory is only possible by the victory over sin and death through Jesus Christ. He is the key. He is the victory. He

John's Vision of the Woman

is the One to whom all knees will bow and tongues confess that He is Lord of all.

But the Book of James writes how faith without works is dead (2:17); so too is spiritual warfare if we do not engage in it. We lose the battle without ever firing a shot, and the enemy takes territory and drowns these regions and the lives of those who inhabit these spaces in darkness.

Michael does not sit on the sidelines. As the only named archangel in canon Scripture he is granted vast power by God, but never forget that we are also granted this power through the baptism and indwelling of the Holy Spirit. It is not by our might but by the Spirit of the Lord!

I believe this is a vastly overlooked result that many Christians are aware of but do not take to heart.

Michael defeats Satan in combat.

Read that again.

Michael, the archangel, and his angels defeat Satan and his angels. Not God, Jesus, or the Holy Spirit. Michael.

If we are empowered with the Holy Spirit and rooted in the knowledge and wisdom of the Word of God, then we too are able to overcome the enemy. But this is not a one-punch knockout scenario. This is continuous warfare. This is a battle in the trenches.

As Christians we are called to be continuously praying, continuously fasting, continuously being in the Bible. Why? So that we are empowered and able to defeat the devil and his army.

If we do not do the things the Scriptures tell us to do in spiritual warfare, then we are powerless and useless in the fight.

Christians, especially those who live through the end-times, must be aware of the spiritual battle that is manifesting itself through physical means.

The rabid antisemitism that has spread worldwide since the October 7 massacre,[2] I believe, is prophetic in nature and is fulfilling the biblical prophecy of the world turning against Israel.

All because Israel is defending itself against demonically driven terrorists who worship death and commit atrocities that make Satan proud. Why? Because they are committed against God's chosen people.

This is evidenced in the continued persecution the woman suffers at the hands of the dragon: "When the dragon saw that he was cast down to the earth, he persecuted the woman who gave birth to the male Child. The woman was given two wings of a great eagle, that she might fly into the wilderness...where she is to be nourished" (Rev. 12:13–14, MEV).

As the church of Jesus Christ is brought into the fold of salvation, so too is the enmity of Satan and his forces aimed at the bride of Christ and Israel. They are targeted in coordinated strikes aimed at bringing about division between the two of them, yet they are both treasured by the Lord and Savior, Jesus Christ.

It is so important for Christians to understand the deep love God has not only for them but also for the descendants of Abraham. It is why the Father sent the Son to die for us all.

Did Jesus fulfill the Law? Yes, a hundred times yes. But the Abrahamic covenant is still firmly in place and shall be until this era is done with and there is a new heaven and a new earth.

Far, far, far too many who claim to be Christians hold venomous hatred of the Jews,[3] and this is wrong from a biblical standard. This hatred of Israel comes from one place, and one place only: the deceptive mind of Satan.

This hatred Satan has for Israel is shown again in the vision John is receiving with the dragon pursuing the woman. He will not simply let her go. And why is that? Because of how important she is to God and to His plan of salvation for the world.

But John sees—as we all should, as he saw in life—that even

in the face of persecution God offers protection and respite from the assault of the dragon. This enrages Satan to no end: being thwarted over and over, constantly reminded of his folly (challenging God) and knowing that he can never overcome the Lord and that his time left is fleeting.

Satan, as John states in his vision, is unrelenting in his persecution of Israel and Christians (v. 17). Antisemitism and anti-Christian social views, discrimination, persecution, laws, and sentiments will increase (and are increasing) into the end-times. Israel is surrounded by her enemies and has made even more on the world stage.

Aside from the remnant, a large portion of the Christian church has been seduced and deceived by the love of money, radical sexual and gender ideologies, political blindness, and comfort and has lost her zeal for the Lord.

When either of these two groups takes a stand against the world in different ways, they will be targeted with severe prejudice. However, the world will only continue to get worse if those who believe in the one true God stand on the sidelines doing nothing. Thus, each group—Israel and Christians—needs spiritual strength and to lean into the Lord to endure the attacks of the dragon.

CHAPTER 13

The BEAST from the SEA

IMAGINE BEING JOHN at this moment, going from vision to vision, witnessing events no human in history has ever seen or ever will (at least in this fashion).

Imagine trying to make sense of these things on our own. It's impossible! People are still arguing about the meanings of the signs John wrote about, but thankfully he had the guidance and discernment of the Holy Spirit.

Imagine being in and knowing you are in the spirit realm and experiencing "jumps," like the one going from Revelation chapters 12 to 13.

You'd go from being in places like the throne room of God to seeing massive objects crash onto the earth to being on a beach with sand and watching in awe—or even some fear at such a sight—as a beast rises out of the water. This is not the awe or wonder of something beautiful, but something terrifying and evil.

There is so much symbolism in this chapter and in the description of the beasts within it.

> I saw a beast rising up out of the sea, having seven heads and ten horns, and on his horns ten crowns, and on his heads a blasphemous name....His feet were like the feet of a bear....The dragon gave him his power....And I saw one of his heads as if it had been mortally wounded, and his deadly wound was healed. And all the world marveled and followed the beast....
>
> Then I saw another beast coming up out of the earth, and he had two horns like a lamb and spoke like a dragon.
>
> —REVELATION 13:1–3, 11

The Beast from the Sea

From the limbs of the first beast rising out of the sea to the horns and crowns that adorn his head, all authority and power granted to this future leader is conditional and limited.

All that these beasts, including the dragon, seek is merely an imitation of the true power and authority wielded by the Lord God Almighty.

Even the wound on the beast's head is a mock injury compared to the nails driven into Jesus' hands and feet, the crown of thorns pressed upon His head, and the piercing of His side.

Nothing about Satan is original. It is all a twisted and corrupt version of God's creation and design. Satan, that foul dragon, is incapable of creation, so he must warp that which God did create into a perverse version of what it was intended to be.

Satan does all this, granting the beast power and corrupting God's creation, in a vain attempt to replace God and chase his futile, narcissistic belief (which saw him expelled from paradise) that he is somehow able to replace God.

In vanity this beast will deceive the people of the earth to worship him, and he will succeed.

Take notice of the wording used frequently throughout this chapter. John repeatedly uses the word *blaspheme* or *blasphemy* to describe the words and actions committed by the beast and, by extension, his followers.

The definition of *blasphemy*, according to Oxford (until they decide to change the meaning of this word, like so many other words have been changed in recent years to conform to radical agendas), is "the action or offence of speaking sacrilegiously about God or sacred things; profane talk."[1]

Fellow Christians, we must know the Word of God inside and out so that we may recognize this type of talk in our own society before this end of days begins. We are already witnessing profane talk against the Lord. It is no longer the fringe of society doing this, but the highest levels of leadership in every sector of society.

We are witnessing in these days of preparation demonic, pagan statues being erected across the United States, even inside state capitol buildings.[2] People are being desensitized to the disrespect and rejection of God on all fronts only to one day worship that which is a false god with no redeeming qualities or path to salvation. The beasts will guide them down a path of death.

When we read these verses, we must understand the significance. The beast is allowed to desecrate much of the earth that still honors and glorifies God (v. 7). God allows this; if He did not, it would not happen.

This time of mass persecution must take place under a system that will allow it to occur, in which every country bows and yields to the power granted to the beast. For this to happen there must be a world system implemented. Countries will yield their sovereignty to the globalist agenda.

The world is witnessing the push for this system to be implemented this very day! For the life of me I cannot understand why so many Christians refuse to recognize biblical prophecy taking place in the world today, but for one reason: a lack of biblical knowledge and discernment.

Environmental, social, and governance (ESG) scores, digital currencies, restrictions on individual liberties, media censorship, the weaponization of government organizations against their citizens, radical environmental legislation, destruction of systems put in place by God, apostasy within the church—so much is happening in our day and age that is preparing the way for this false trinity to assume control over the earth.

THE FALSE PROPHET

The dragon and the beast are not alone in this vision John is experiencing, but they are joined by the false prophet. These three losers cannot help but continue to try to imitate God's awesome power and the authority and the unity of the Trinity.

> I saw another beast coming up out of the earth, and he had two horns like a lamb....And he...causes the earth and those who dwell in it to worship the first beast.... He performs great signs, so that he even makes fire come down from heaven on the earth in the sight of men.
> —REVELATION 13:11–13

John describes some of the powers given to this false prophet, and he's imitating the actions of Elijah! These three bums saw how Elijah embarrassed their false priests of the Baal principality and executed them for their heresy (1 Kings 18). Now again, like the court magicians of Pharaoh, they are trying to imitate this awesome power with a fake version.

And what will these beings do with such power that has been granted to them? Attack those who have accepted the truth of God's salvation plan. They will put to death those who speak the truth, all so they may continue to promulgate their lie and take as many souls into oblivion as they can.

If they have to suffer for eternity, they want as much company as they can convince to go with them.

This is not some science-fiction fantasy event; this is something that is certain to take place.

Control, control, control. It is all about control. When we see politicians, unelected bureaucrats, and nongovernmental organizations try to assume power that in no way, shape, or form belongs to them,[3] it is all working toward the consolidation of control over the whole earth. That is Satan's objective: to totally take over that which God created and of which He is the Prince.

But spoiler alert: God will not allow this to come to completion. Even as crackdowns are put in place and people without the mark of the beast are hunted down, God is still in control, and these events must take place before He issues correction to the world.

During this time of the beasts, however, the persecution will be unlike anything we see today or will see before their reign. And that is saying something.

Christians in Nigeria are murdered by the thousands;[4] house groups in China are shut down, with members being thrown in jail without due process; a Canadian pastor was hunted down for holding services during COVID by police using a helicopter;[5] the Department of (In)Justice targets conservatives and pro-life groups with a vengeance.[6] But all this will not compare to the deadly persecution of those who turn to God during the great tribulation.

Evil will run rampant in a way we simply cannot fathom. We are shocked and appalled by what we see today in every aspect of society. But during this time, faith in God will come with a physical death sentence. How many Christians today would be willing to pay that price when it doesn't just come knocking but is kicking the door down, guns blazing?

This is the seething hatred Satan has for any who bow before the Lord God Almighty. And John tells us this in no uncertain terms:

> And the dragon was enraged with the woman, and he went to make war with the rest of her offspring, who keep the commandments of God and have the testimony of Jesus Christ.
> —REVELATION 12:17

Waging war against the followers of Jesus, these systems Satan will put in place, all enabled by global networks of control, will lead to the infamous mark of the beast.

It is incredible that we are watching the systems and technologies being developed today that can implement such a world-altering system: biometric scanning systems, microchip technologies that are already being implanted into people's brains and palms, and databases for all the personal information freely handed over by the world's populace.

Don't believe me? Let's take a quick look at just some of the companies using these types of technologies (and pushing for them to become commonplace).

Whole Foods was bought by Amazon in 2017, and since their acquisition they have announced (and begun rolling out) a program to bring biometric payments to all their Whole Foods stores.[7]

With just a wave of your hand a biometric scanner can read your palm signature and pull funds from your account.

According to a report by the *New York Post*, "The technology works by analyzing both a person's unique skin pattern and 'underlying vein structure,' according to the company, and links this 'palm signature' to their Prime account and payment."[8]

The Amazon website claims that a customer's biometric data will not be tracked or used for market research and that they will not provide the government with this information unless legally obliged to do so.[9]

You can believe that if you want, but I certainly do not.

While some people interviewed in the article viewed the scanner with some trepidation, others said they would sign up for it without a second thought.

"I love it. I have no problem with [it] collecting all my information," one female user said. "I don't care. It's just a lot easier. I like that they have all my info so if I want to buy alcohol, I don't have to show my ID."[10]

Ease and comfort over privacy. And she is certainly not alone in this sentiment.

Then, we have Elon Musk's venture, Neuralink.

Let me be up front about this one: I do not believe Musk has nefarious plans for his brain chip company. But that does not mean it cannot be abused by people other than Musk in the future.

At the time of this writing, Neuralink has successfully implanted its first brain chip into a patient, Noland Arbaugh, who is a quadriplegic.

With this new brain chip a new life awaits Arbaugh, as he can now utilize a mouse on a computer and even play some video games with it. He would never have been able to engage in this type of activity without it.

But with people in positions of leadership and influence who seek to control the lives of others around the world, pushing a globalist agenda that requires complete control over the earth's populace, a chip with this type of capability could be used for evil purposes.

Even those without debilitating disabilities are flocking to get chips implanted into their bodies.

Take "Chip Girl," for example. I do not use her real name, which you can easily look up, but I'm not listing it, as a sign I bear this young woman no ill will.[11]

She has gone viral on social media, most notably on TikTok, for having a chip implanted in her hand that was designed and programmed by her tech-savvy husband. With this implant she can unlock the doors to her home as well as drawers within their mansion.

Yes, they are very well to do, but that is not the point.

Oftentimes in our society the lifestyles of the rich and famous are soon imitated by those who do not have the same finances and resources available to them. You know, the trendsetters.

With around five million followers on TikTok and hundreds

of thousands on other social apps, it is clear she has influenced many with positive feelings toward implanting technology in their bodies.

Chip Girl's husband has an even more advanced version of her hand chip, and his is able to access a wide range of information such as social media accounts and websites.

Herein lies the danger of mixing technology and the human body.

John tells us that while the beast has the authority to and will kill those who do not bow the knee to him, there will also be a system in place that will allow him to implement the mark of the beast on the entire world, as John writes:

> He causes all, both small and great, rich and poor, free and slave, to receive a mark on their right hand or on their foreheads, and that no one may buy or sell except one who has the mark or the name of the beast, or the number of his name.
> —REVELATION 13:16–17

That number, as John writes, is 666 (v. 18). We do not yet know the name of the beast.

So how can an event such as barring people from buying and selling be implemented in our increasingly controlled world? This mark will undoubtedly control access to all these avenues of commerce in ways many do not expect.

Currently, we can unlock our phones, which nearly everyone in the world has, with a password or facial recognition.

Online shopping is continually growing, with corporate monsters like Amazon and Walmart dominating the online grocery retail market, according to Statista,[12] and this trend is only expected to grow in the near future.

When I go shopping at Walmart, usually on Saturday mornings to avoid the later crowds, there are just as many employees shopping for online orders as there are actual customers in the store. There are rarely more than two employees manning registers, and that number is usually one.

I firmly believe this is because eventually the only people shopping inside a Walmart will be employees.

Notice how businesses like Walgreens have begun locking up all their items due to the massive increase in theft in places like California and New York because criminals suffer zero repercussions for stealing.[13]

So how do you prevent theft and attain absolute control over your product? Locking the doors and making online orders the mandatory way of ordering food.

With a system such as the one needed to implement the mark of the beast, users can be approved or denied based on their status with the mark.

Access to phones will be controlled by the few corporate entities that offer these services. We are already seeing the propaganda machine that is the mainstream media manipulate what it considers "news," which is simply social messaging to control the thought patterns of those who watch it.

Understand, these words of warning about the coming control under the beast are not my words; this is what the Bible says. It will happen. We can only surmise what this will look like, but if the signs of the times we live in are an indication—developing technology such as AI, and the acceptance of censorship by many societies in the world for a false sense of security—then we are well on our way to developing the system of the mark of the beast.

In these days, control will be nearly total. Internet access, banking access, food ordering, online ordering, and digital assets will all be controlled. By then even cars will be controlled, considering how digitized they have become. Mechanics for many modern models almost need a computer engineering degree to work on them (looking at you, BMW).

As the days advance toward the future John is shown and warns us about, Jesus tells us what to do in the meantime.

Yes, we are to love the Lord our God with all our hearts, souls, and minds and to love our neighbors as ourselves, but there is another command specifically for Christians in our day and age that Jesus gave to His followers: to watch for His return.

For all the examples and times Jesus told His disciples to watch for the signs of His return, I will go with the parable of the ten virgins in Matthew 25, coincidentally in the chapter right after Jesus discusses the signs of His return and the endtimes in Matthew 24.

Within this story of the wise and the foolish virgins those who were not prepared and were not watching for the bridegroom were left out of the wedding, even though they believed he would one day come. They had their lamps, so it appeared from the outside they were ready, but inside they were missing oil to light their lamps. They were not prepared, nor were their hearts in the right place.

Jesus closes the parable with this command:

> Watch therefore, for you know neither the day nor the hour in which the Son of Man is coming.
> —MATTHEW 25:13

This is, of course, not the only time Jesus commands those who hail Him as the Messiah to watch, but the fact remains the same: We as Christians are called to watch for the signs of His return and, in the meantime, preach the gospel message that has the power to save humanity from the eternal death that awaits those who do not accept Jesus Christ as Lord.

It takes Holy Spirit guidance and discernment to understand the times we live in and to look at the world through a biblical lens. This is why it is so, so, so important to spend time in prayer, fasting, reading the Bible, and in community with one another so that we may grow closer to Him and stronger in our faith!

Because one day, there will be those on earth who will face one of two choices: choose eternal life with Jesus and be physically killed for it, or take the mark of the beast and face eternal death for it.

Sadly, we know many will be deceived and take the mark, but in the meantime it is our duty as Christians to spread the good word of Jesus to as much of the world as we possibly can.

CHAPTER 14

The LAMB, the 144,000, and the REAPING

WITH GOD, JOHN knew there were no coincidences, only purpose. As we've read about in Revelation 7, God sealed (marked) His people—12,000 from each of the twelve tribes of Israel, numbering 144,000 in total.

We have sadly seen many cult leaders use these verses of Scripture to assume the mantle meant for Jesus Christ, and Him alone, as well as to tell their followers they are a part of the 144,000—such as the recently convicted "cult mom," Lori Vallow, for example. She, along with her husband, Chad Daybell, murdered her two children.[1]

Daybell was a doomsday cultist as part of an offshoot of Mormonism. Lori believed she was a member of the 144,000 and, I quote, "assigned to carry out the work of the 144,000 at Christ's second coming," while believing she was some sort of goddess who had supernatural powers.[2]

Folks, demons are real, and they do not want the truth of Jesus Christ to spread around the world. They know there is power in that name, and they must submit to that power.

Jesus did, of course, bridge the gap for Gentiles to be brought before the Lord in righteousness, washed by the blood of the Lamb. Yet even Jesus said He came for the Jews when talking with the Samaritan woman in John 4.

Thank the Lord He fused our Gentile branches into the tree of salvation along with Israel, not in place of Israel.

It is so, so important not to forget the Jewishness of Jesus. For decades, perhaps centuries, Christians have neglected to study the Law under the false assumption that it no longer matters with Christ's resurrection and Paul's writings in the New Testament.

But it still holds immense importance to the lives of Christians and Jews alike. It opens our eyes to God's righteousness and His morality—what He deems moral and immoral. Even Jesus willingly submitted Himself to the Law in life, and His death and resurrection brought the fulfillment of the Law, not the discarding of it.

As the ultimate sacrifice, Jesus bridged the gap between God and mankind with His precious blood. He is the final sacrifice needed for salvation and the absolving of sins, but that does not make the Ten Commandments irrelevant. Quite the opposite, since the life Jesus led was blameless because He abided by God's Law and commandments.

There is no shame in struggling with figuring out where a Gentile stands when it comes to the Law. The Law was given to the nation of Israel because they are God's people, chosen and set apart. But by being grafted into the tree of salvation, as Paul writes about in Romans 11, there is a clear separation in future paths and prophecies for the nation of Israel and the body of Christ.

Thankfully, salvation is offered to all, as are callings, purposes, and gifts from the Lord Most High. One such calling is for the 144,000 of the Lamb who are marked by God.

Outside of the twelve disciples, these chosen are the closest Jesus will have to an entourage. They are set apart, redeemed for a special, specific purpose.

John is able to discern their great importance, almost as though they are the priests of the Lamb, much like the Levites were given their special place as the priests of God.

And special is the place for these chosen. They get to sing a song of praise and worship before the throne of God, which no one else can learn but them. What a great honor that is, to present before the Lord an offering none outside of the 144,000 can bring before Him.

Color me jealous (but not really—"thou shalt not covet" and all).

Reading through their qualifications makes me think even more of the Levites, of how their lives were offered up as sacrifices before God, and they had certain restrictions placed upon them so that they could maintain their righteousness in service of the Lord (Num. 18).

So too do the 144,000 have this righteousness, if not even more so!

> These are the ones who were not defiled with women, for they are virgins. These are the ones who follow the Lamb wherever He goes. These were redeemed from among men, being firstfruits to God and to the Lamb. And in their mouth was found no deceit, for they are without fault before the throne of God.
> —REVELATION 14:4–5

If the Lord found their purity so important to list it in the Bible, then we should pay attention! God values the righteous lives that we live and the effort we put forth in honoring His commands, design, and purpose.

We are made righteous in Him, and while we can never live perfect lives in this sin-cursed world, we can certainly put forth the effort. We may stumble, we may even fall, but we have the choice, just as Paul did, to continue running the race, to not allow the word *quit* to enter our minds and to press on, having faith in Him and not our own powers and abilities.

As I read these introductory verses in Revelation 14, I also think of Cain and Abel.

Abel brought the Lord his very best, the firstfruits of his flock, and the Lord found this to be an acceptable offering that was brought before Him. As we all know (I assume), Cain did not bring an offering suitable to the Lord and was rejected for it.

These 144,000 are found to be acceptable before the Lord,

and this is why they are lined up with the Lamb, the perfect sacrifice for the sins of the world. King Jesus will have His own purified priests in His church, and the lack of fault found within this group that has been set apart makes me think that these are the priests of Jesus' reign.

John uses a word quite often here, which in English is *then*. But in the Greek the word is *kai*, which is more accurately translated as "and." There is so much happening that John is trying to describe; he's going, "Then, this happened. Then, this happened. Then, I saw this. Then, another angel. Then, then, then. Kai, kai, kai. And, and, and."

John is witnessing a lot!

Think about how you would react to all this. Then, after seeing the Lamb of God with 144,000 of His sealed and marked followers, three angels take to the sky with proclamations (vv. 6–9). I have to admit, I would be in awe of a lot of what I saw and would probably have my jaw hanging open, trying to take it all in!

Like all the angels John has witnessed in the angelic-filled vision, these appear with purpose (as all things of the Lord have purpose) and bring with them a message for John to hear.

John witnesses the first angel, who has been selected by God to make a proclamation. Notice how even though the words of these angels are very important, John's language is different when talking about them.

His reference to the flying angels simply states what it is they are doing and the powerful messages they bring with them. This leads me to the belief that they are messenger angels, not warriors.

So far in the Book of Revelation we have seen and read several instances when John makes it a priority to point out a *mighty* angel. He appears able to discern the levels of hierarchy within the angelic ranks, something that makes perfect sense— not just for one of the twelve disciples but for the man entrusted with the Revelation of Jesus Christ.

The message brought by the first angel is exhorting all humanity—every nation, tribe, tongue, and people—offering another exhortation in a long list of warnings from the Bible that the hour of God's judgment is upon the earth.

I find it very odd how many Christians do not put much stock in the multitude of warnings from the Bible that beseech people to be ready for the day of the Lord. This is not so people live in a constant state of fear; on the contrary, we are to live with expectation for the day Jesus returns!

There is hope in Jesus Christ, so as we watch the world devolve around us, we do not live in a state of fear, depression, or anxiety. We live in a state of victory because Jesus has overcome sin and death, and He will come back as the King of kings and Lord of lords.

However, the second angel has such a deep and impactful message, considering it only takes up one verse in the Bible:

> Babylon is fallen, is fallen, that great city, because she has made all nations drink of the wine of the wrath of her fornication.
> —REVELATION 14:8

When the angel declares this, I cannot help but read this verse and think of the current state of America. Yes, there is much more to the world than the United States, but as a resident and veteran of the US, it pains me to see not just the state of morality but also the spiritual decay that has occurred in this country.

While Babylon was a real place in history and was even used to bring judgment upon ancient Israel, it has also manifested as the spirit of Babylon throughout history. Many cities, states, and nations have accepted the spirit of Babylon and, in doing so, have brought God's judgment upon their people.

Babylon controls regions, much as did the prince of Persia,

who held up the angelic messenger sent to answer Daniel (Dan. 10). (I know many believe this messenger was Gabriel; however, I am not in that group. Daniel recognized Gabriel in a previous vision, and the angel says he warred with the prince of Persia. But that's another discussion for another time.)

By taking up residence in various nations throughout history, Babylon is a principality and power of darkness. Vast areas of the earth have fallen to the influence of Babylon, and when we look at descriptions of Babylon throughout Revelation, we see it referred to in the feminine. Drunkenness is involved, as well as sexual immorality and fornication.

These fallen nations—much like the kingdoms of Babylon under the reign of Nebuchadnezzar, Persia, and Rome—suffered for their embrace of false gods and idols. Think of these once-great nations, then fast-forward to the superpower of today: the United States of America.

How much greater are the sins of a nation with over three hundred million citizens than the ancient cities of old? How many more idols, child sacrifices, immoralities, and faithless are there in the modern world?

The sins against God in today's age are on a scale that was simply impossible in the ancient pagan world.

It should come as no surprise to Christians who read the Bible and discern the actions taking place within the United States (and, to a larger extent, the whole world) that God's mercy does not run out, but He brings it to an end, and a period of judgment is loosed upon the unrepentant.

The world's sin grieves our holy God, and as the proclamation that Babylon the principality has fallen does, so too does the third angel's decree spell out the fate of those who bowed down to the beast and false prophet.

By taking the mark of the beast people are signing their own death sentence—an eternal death sentence. They are aligning themselves squarely against the Lord of hosts and choosing the kingdom of darkness over His kingdom of life. This choosing of the cup of Babylon and rejecting the waters of life that God offers to all opens the gates of God's wrath upon the people who chose eternal death over salvation.

It's not just making a choice of evil over good, though; taking this mark is so much more than that. It is an insult to God. It is a metaphorical spitting in His face and mockery of Him and His creation and design for humanity.

Paul gives us a prophetic warning in Galatians 6:7–8 of these events that are to come. He warns us, saying, "Do not be deceived, God is not mocked; for whatever a man sows, that he will also reap. For he who sows to his flesh will of the flesh reap corruption, but he who sows to the Spirit will of the Spirit reap everlasting life."

These judgments are the culmination of God's patience and mercy to a sinful world coming to an end, and the next part of the chapter highlights the final harvest (Rev. 14:15–20), which falls in line with the words given to Paul.

Bear in mind there are many seasons of planting, sowing, and harvesting. We see it in the mission field, in evangelistic outreaches, in the stirring of revivals—when moments souls long prayed for finally awaken to the call of salvation. Some have been lifted in prayer for days, others for months, years, even decades, as the faithful intercede without ceasing, refusing to surrender hope. This is the rhythm of God's kingdom—the labor of love, the patient endurance, the unseen hand of the Almighty bringing forth the harvest in its appointed time. And as Revelation 14 reminds us, the ultimate harvest is coming, a day when every seed sown will yield its eternal fruit. The only question that remains is: When that day comes, where will you stand?

CHAPTER 15

The LEAD-UP to the BOWL JUDGMENTS

JOHN KNOWS FINALITY is found within the angels administering the bowls of the wrath of God. As great as Satan's hatred toward God is, it pales in comparison to the Lord's wrath and His righteous anger at having sin introduced into the world He created.

People ask the question, "Well, why doesn't God do something about it?" Well, He has been doing something about it, and this "thing" He is doing has been in His time frame, not ours.

These judgments come into fruition according to His will, not ours. And all shall see what happens when He finally does "something" about it and brings an end to sin and death in this sin-cursed world.

Up until these bowls of judgment, God has been showing us mercy, grace, and love. Oh, how quickly we forget that each and every person who has sinned is deserving of death, but instead our loving Father has offered us the chance of salvation and having our sins washed away, making us as white as snow before His throne of judgment.

What a sight John has witnessed during his time in the Spirit to this point. Again, he witnesses untold numbers of saints, armed with "harps of God," lifting up praise and worship to God (Rev. 15:2–4).

I continue to maintain that the Book of Revelation is a book of praise on the same level as the Book of Psalms. There is so much praise and worship and adoration of God within this vision John receives that we as His followers must take notice

The Lead-Up to the Bowl Judgments

and understand just how important our offering up praise and worship to the Master of the universe truly is!

John is introduced to a level of worship and intimacy with God during the Revelation that no other person has ever witnessed in this life. Angels and saints, those set aside, and all creation praise the Lord for John to witness and attest to the greatness of God.

Reading about how God prepares the angels of heaven before pouring out His wrath, it is clear He has a season of preparation before everything, including our lives!

Gideon had to conduct preparations before overcoming the Midianites (Judg. 7), David spent years of preparation and trial before ever becoming king, the disciples prepared for their ministry after Jesus during His time on earth, and Jesus Himself prepared His entire life to give His life up for us on the cross.

I read this, and it is crystal clear in the Scriptures that God is not a brash God. He is ever-patient, and there is order in all things that He does. In that order is preparation. And the preparation John sees amid a sea of glass and fire (how cool would that be to see?) is worship! Praise!

> And I saw something like a sea of glass mingled with fire, and those who have the victory over the beast... standing on the sea of glass, having harps of God. They sing the song of Moses.
> —REVELATION 15:2–3

The saints are singing in victory the song of Moses. Look, I cannot state enough how important national Israel is to the Lord. We—Christians, the church—are the bride of Jesus Christ, and yes, of course, we hold a dear and special place as the ones who are granted salvation and will reign with Christ for eternity. But it is the song of Moses (Exod. 15) sung with the song of the Lamb that brings total victory over the beast and all things related to him.

The song of Moses and the song of the Lamb come together perfectly, to me, as the grafting together, not the replacement, of Judaism and Christianity. Side by side, united by the blood of the Lamb, they offer salvation to God's people.

It makes perfect sense.

The way John describes the angels of God's wrath, they are most assuredly trusted and set apart by God, but they do not appear to be warrior-angels such as Michael or the great and mighty angels John describes earlier in Revelation. Their garb is that of priests, not warriors, and this implies that the action of pouring out the bowls of God's judgment is, in fact, a holy act, with them being set aside and consecrated (Rev. 15:6).

They come out of the temple John sees in the vision and are ceremoniously given the bowls of judgment from one of the living creatures, though we do not know which (v. 7).

We read this and realize these are sanctified creatures, just as we are. They are performing a ceremony much like the priests of the Old Testament when offering up sacrifices before the Lord. Except now the earth is being cleansed of its sin in a way that the Lord has deemed necessary for the corruption that has taken over.

There is great significance in the manifest presence (the smoke) of the Lord (v. 8). This is what sanctifies the angels to perform their holy duties. The same smoke led Israel as a cloud during the day and was represented as a burning bush before Moses (Exod. 3). Wherever we find the presence of the Lord, we find holiness and consecration.

This is the same smoke that filled Solomon's temple for the Lord (1 Kings 8). Each time, no one could endure being in the smoke of the almighty God.

Perhaps we have lost the reverence the presence of God truly deserves. Yes, we have been gifted the indwelling of the Holy

Spirit into our very lives, but have we gotten to a point where we either take it for granted or do not value it at all?

Do we consecrate ourselves, as our bodies are the temples of the Holy Spirit, by living out our lives in obedience to God's Word? Or do we partake in actions and say words that desecrate this temple?

I can say from a personal perspective, there is always more I can do to go deeper in my relationship with the Lord. I do not mean in a religious way where I feel forced to do such a thing or I'm not a good enough Christian, but I make a personal choice by continuing to die to my flesh in new ways and striving to live a righteous life to honor and glorify Him, not myself.

THE BOWLS OF JUDGMENT BEGIN

For the end of chapter 15 of this book, I'm also going to include the first verse from Revelation 16, the beginning of the bowls of judgment. This is the final preparation, the final command that sends forth the angels of judgment:

> Then I heard a loud voice from the temple saying to the seven angels, "Go, pour out the bowls of the wrath of God on the earth."
> —REVELATION 16:1, MEV

When I read this verse, it is here that all the false prophets and teachers who have tried to say the world is ending are proved wrong.

There is such a finality in the command coming from the temple in heaven. Whether it is God's voice or not is up for debate; the impression I get from reading it is that John would identify the voice of God instead of just a loud voice. Additionally, he refers to the wrath of God in the third person and does not address the wrath as "My wrath," for example, "My wrath upon the earth."

As this chapter begins we must remember that this is what true justice looks like. There is no going back for the earth, nay, all creation. God has suffered sin for long enough, and now, according to His timeline, the earth and those who dwell in it and worship the beast must pay the price, even though there is still much to be done after the bowl judgments.

At long last John witnesses God's righteous judgment on the beast and his followers on the earth. His spiritual maturity and relationship with the Lord are so strong that he does not write about being in awe of the bowls being poured out over the earth, for he knew this day would come.

As mankind blasphemes the Lord in the midst of their torment, they are reaping exactly what they have sown. I say *they* because I have no plans to be there!

But John knows that the Lord is holy, and He cannot, and will not, tolerate sin. As God says, "Vengeance is Mine" (Deut. 32:35; Rom. 12:19).

Well, we've finally arrived at the time of vengeance upon the earth.

When you look over the bowl judgments, one very glaring similarity should stick out to us as we see just what the Lord has planned for the earth, and that is the similarities to the plagues wrought upon Egypt when Moses told Pharaoh to let God's people go.

Let's take a look at the plagues that struck Egypt in the Old Testament (Exod. 7–12):

1. The waters of Egypt turned to blood—all waters, including those in pitchers and buckets. Fish died, a stench rose from the river, and the water was undrinkable.

2. Frogs plagued the land of Egypt, and when they died, the land again stank from the death in Egypt.

3. Lice afflicted the people and animals of Egypt. Immense levels of discomfort and mental anguish would accompany such a plague.

4. Swarms of flies were released against Egypt, but none affected the Hebrews in the land of Goshen, a refuge set aside for them by the Lord.

5. The livestock were struck. This did not just cover cows, but horses, donkeys, camels, oxen, and sheep. All types of herd animals were afflicted by the plague, except for those of Israel.

6. A plague of boils drove people mad with the discomfort, living in a state without any peace.

7. Hail rained down on Egypt. This economically devastating plague destroyed crops as well as those who were still in the fields when it rained down from heaven. But this is not the cold type of hail that we see during weather events; this hail brought with it God's fire upon the land. Destruction literally rained down from the sky, except in the land of Goshen.

8. Locusts covered the land of Egypt. Imagine locusts everywhere you go, inside and outside. In your home, on all your things, when you try to use the bathroom! Everywhere! By now I would be calling for Pharaoh to get rid of these Hebrews and beg for God's forgiveness.

9. Darkness enveloped the land. So deep was this darkness that people stayed inside because they could not see anything outside. Yet again, this plague did not affect Israel, who had light within their dwellings.

10. Finally, the deaths of the firstborn. God has proved time and time again that He tries to get our and others' attention before He uses death to accomplish His goals. This plague started the Jewish holiday of Passover and foreshadows the sacrifice of the Lamb of God, which saves us from death.

Now, before we go through the rest of chapter 16, let's list the judgments that will befall the world in comparison to the plagues that tormented the people of Egypt. (See Revelation 16.)

- Foul and loathsome sores afflict people.
- Seas made up of salt water turn to blood.
- Freshwater lakes and rivers turn to blood.
- Mankind is scorched by the sun.
- Darkness and pain fill the beast's kingdom.
- The river Euphrates dries up, paving the way for Armageddon.
- The earth is utterly shaken.

When we look at these two very separate events, we see some striking similarities.

Blood, sores, darkness—why do so many view the plagues of Egypt as a literal event but are hesitant to admit that much of the vision John receives in Revelation holds both a metaphorical, allegorical meaning and a meaning as a literal series of events that will strike the earth?

Each time, the Lord turns water into blood, and a stench and death come with it. People are afflicted with sores and are deeply, physically, and mentally uncomfortable from this. Darkness envelops the area, sowing chaos in its wake.

While the plagues of Egypt served the purpose of showcasing

God's ultimate power and releasing His chosen people from bondage, these end-times judgments are of a very different manner.

God has brought judgments upon different societies and His people Israel at different points throughout history as a means to drive them toward repentance and back into a righteous way of living in our covenant life with Him.

These bowls do not represent punishment in the hopes that forgiveness will come out of it.

This is God's judgment finalizing the ending season of the earth. This is His wrath poured out over the beast, the false prophet, and those who took his sign, rejecting God and damning themselves for eternity.

The Lord's long-suffering and His redemption plan are in their final hours, as it has been thousands of years that He has shown grace, love, and mercy in response to the hubris of mankind.

But notice that even as the bowls are poured out for John to see, this is still a season of preparation, preparation for the return of Jesus Christ as the mighty Warrior-King in the bowls being poured out, for none who worship the beast will reign with Him.

CHAPTER 16

The BOWLS of GOD'S JUDGMENT

This next chapter of Revelation unveils one of the most terrifying and sobering moments in all Scripture: the outpouring of the seven bowls of God's wrath. These judgments are not merely symbolic; they represent the full and final measure of divine retribution upon a world that has defiantly rejected God.

Unlike the previous judgments seen in the seals and trumpets, which were partial in scope, these plagues are total and irreversible. Here, we finally see that God's patience has come to an end and the day of reckoning has arrived. The wicked, who have hardened their hearts and pledged allegiance to the beast, will now drink the full cup of God's fury.

The time for repentance has passed, and the world must now face the righteous judgment of the Almighty.

THE FIRST BOWL: FOUL AND LOATHSOME SORES

People who accept the mark of the beast and worship at his altar have opened themselves up to not just spiritual damnation; they have offered up their bodies and minds as well. They allow a stronghold over their person, and they become enemies of God. Sadly, this is by their own decision-making.

Note that as we read about *foul* sores, we should consider what would accompany such an affliction: a stench, just like the rivers of Egypt that turned to blood. Everywhere you'd go, you'd smell it. A foul wound is also one that will ooze with some type of liquid, perhaps pus, or it just leaks. Gross, I know, but this is what John sees, and it is important enough to be put into the holy Word of God, so I believe this makes it a worthy topic of discussion.

There is a level of physical grossness, an "ick" factor if you will, that will start off these judgments, and it is representative of the death and decay that awaits those who have rejected God's offer of salvation. A foul sore is so deeply representative of the spiritual decay that has taken place over the world, and now God's timeline has entered into the period of eliminating the contamination.

One of the most challenging aspects for us to understand in Revelation is the reality that when God's wrath is poured out, it falls upon all who have taken the mark of the beast—men, women, and children. This leads to some pretty difficult questions: What happens to children who are forced to take the mark? Are they held accountable for a choice they did not make? If salvation is impossible for those who receive it (Rev. 14:9–11), does that mean even the innocent are condemned? And if so, how does that align with God's justice and mercy?

Revelation 13:16 says, "He causes all, both small and great, rich and poor, free and slave, to receive a mark on their right hand or on their foreheads." This reinforces the idea that the judgment described in Revelation 16:2—the "harmful and painful sores" that will come upon "the people who bore the mark of the beast and worshiped its image" (ESV)—will reach all levels of society. The Greek words used in the phrase "both small and great" are *mikros* and *megas*, literally meaning "small" and "great" respectively, often referring to both social status and age.[1] This tells us no one who bears the mark is exempt from judgment, raising further questions: Is there an age of accountability in this scenario? Could God extend mercy to those who were coerced? Or does this mark signify an irreversible spiritual state for all who bear it, regardless of circumstances?

While these are difficult questions, Scripture does provide

precedent for entire families suffering judgment due to the sins of their parents. In Numbers 16 Korah, Dathan, and Abiram led a rebellion against Moses, and as a result, the ground opened up and swallowed not only them but also their wives and children (vv. 31–33). This shows that, at times, God's judgment has fallen collectively upon households when the head of the family led them into rebellion.

Could a similar principle apply in these final days, when entire families align themselves with the Antichrist's system? These are weighty considerations that many others far more intelligent than I am have wrestled with for centuries, but these questions do challenge us to trust in God's perfect justice, even when the full answers are beyond our grasp.

Understand, people are going to be tormented day and night by these sores! And sadly, children are going to be afflicted as well. How many parents do you think will force their children, from toddlers to teenagers, to take the mark of the beast?

Imagine now the sight of children crying from this affliction; I cannot help but think of those poor children who are being forced into radical gender-manipulating practices.[2] Irreversible puberty blockers and chemical castrations are forced upon thousands of children in our current day. How much worse will things be when the Lord finally orders the bowls of His judgment onto the earth?

As the human race we truly have much to repent of, but far too many are instead trying to live comfortably in the shadows of an evil society.

It is possible that, like the plagues of Egypt, each bowl judgment dissipates before the next one begins. If that is the case, the sores inflicted by the first bowl may fade over time, only for a fresh outbreak to afflict the world when the fifth bowl is poured out. This would mean each judgment is distinct yet equally devastating, with each wave of suffering serving as a renewed opportunity for repentance.

However, Revelation 16:11 suggests a different reality: that these plagues are cumulative and do not simply vanish. The verse states, "They blasphemed the God of heaven because of *their pains and their sores*, and did not repent of *their deeds*" (emphasis added). This indicates that when the fifth bowl of darkness is poured out (in verses 10 and 11), the sores from the first bowl are still tormenting people. Rather than experiencing temporary afflictions, humanity is subjected to a relentless and compounding judgment. Their suffering does not soften their hearts; instead, they respond with further rebellion, cursing God rather than turning to Him in repentance.

With each succeeding bowl being poured out the earth's discomfort and pain grow greater and greater. Their sores cannot be healed by any treatment or vaccine, which may very well be peddled out as a cure to God's judgment, but to no avail.

With an outbreak that affects the entire world of the beast, and with the days we live in now, it would be prudent to think that a disinformation campaign would accompany such an event to twist the narrative away from God and further deceive the people of the earth.

Medical supplies used to deal with this will dry up, from creams and lotions to stop the smell and oozing to bandages and gauze pads used in vain to clean up these sores. They will fill trash cans and may even be designated as biohazards, creating even more chaos for the world, as every single neighborhood trash collector will have to deal with a large number of these items.

Chaos is going to reign with just the first bowl being poured out. But there is still so much more to follow; we cannot truly understand and comprehend the level of upheaval in society that is going to come upon the earth.

THE SECOND BOWL: OCEANS TURN TO BLOOD

While this is a relatively short summary of the second bowl of judgment, it brings a massive impact upon the world, as essentially death is poured out upon the world's oceans: "Then the second angel poured out his bowl on the sea, and it became blood as of a dead man; and every living creature in the sea died" (v. 3).

I feel it is important to note that those in the "climate cults" of today (who erroneously think raising taxes and eliminating cars and cows will affect the earth) think they know how the earth is going to end.

Read the Bible, folks, and you will see how the world is going to end.

And let me just say that as those who have been given dominion over the earth, we have not done the best job of taking care of it. *Conservation* should not be a word attributed to those who are deceived and worship the earth, but instead should be a serious responsibility for Christians and all residents of this world. This world is a gift from God, and we see His glory and splendor in nature.

You may think this is a repetitive event, since the trumpets have already turned much of the waters in the world into blood. But again, these bowls of judgment are not calls to repentance; that time has passed. Now they are events of totality, affecting all the earth's waters, which are the source of life on the planet.

According to the world's foremost scientific organizations, such as NASA and *PNAS* (*Proceedings of the National Academy of Sciences*, a journal of the National Academy of Sciences), water is the most essential element needed for a planet to have life.[3] So if the Lord removes this life-giving liquid, then He is planning on bringing death to the planet, which we will see shortly, further into Revelation.

Looking extinction in the face, the severe economic, social, and political impact of losing the seas of the earth seems almost trivial but will throw the already chaotic world into even more turmoil.

People are already trying to live in a world where they suffer every moment from foul and ruinous sores. Now the earth just lost the use of her oceans as well as the marine life that lives within them, cutting off essential streams of food and energy production.

Do not think for one second that the oil rigs, which drill in the oceans, will continue to be able to operate in these conditions, leading to an energy crisis on top of everything else.

When the Bible, the Word of God, tells us that the wages of sin is death, we really, *really* need to take Him at His Word.

> For the wages of sin is death, but the gift of God is eternal life in Christ Jesus our Lord.
> —Romans 6:23

THE THIRD BOWL: FRESH WATER IS TURNED TO BLOOD

Blood is the river of life that flows through each and every one of us. It carries oxygen throughout our bodies, and if we lose too much of it, we die.

But take note that it is not the life-giving, vibrant red blood we see when we cut ourselves that stems from the second bowl being poured out. It is described as the "blood of a dead man" (Rev. 16:3, MEV). So picture that dark red and, according to the book of Exodus, putrid-smelling blood that will be the death knell for this world's fresh water.

Imagine a day when someone goes to turn on the water faucet to brush their teeth—irritable and in pain due to the sores affecting their body, scanning the mark on either their face or forehead to order more ointment in the hopes of offering some sort of relief for the sores—and putrid blood pours out of the faucet.

The oceans turning to blood will bring so much chaos and death, and it will affect much more than water, but fresh water turning to blood will bring even more death.

Where will people get the liquid that we need for life? Shelves will be empty within hours, never to be restocked. Of course, people will be hoarding things, as we witnessed with the 2020 pandemic lockdowns.[4] And who knows whatever else the future holds.

But I wonder: Will bottled water be included in the third bowl of judgment? If so, it makes us wonder what the timeline looks like from when the first bowl is poured to when Jesus returns to defeat the armies of the world, or if the bowl judgments will dissipate afterward.

When Satan is imprisoned for a thousand years and Jesus begins His millennial reign, it is logical to assume these afflictions of the world will no longer be in place, even though the new heaven and new earth will have not yet been established. Yet while the earth is enduring God's wrath, life is going to be unbearable. The most basic commodities and acts of survival will take monumental effort.

What makes this judgment stand out, even compared to the similar one over the oceans, is the fact that it wipes out the world's freshwater supply, the very thing people rely on to survive. As discussed earlier, this isn't just a physical catastrophe; it also carries a deeper meaning, serving as a direct response to the bloodshed of God's saints.

John again hears praise to the Lord from an angel. God has repaid the deaths of His saints and prophets with the blood of those who killed them (vv. 5–6).

Blood for blood, life for life.

These verses explain to us how God is absolutely justified in what some view as His "harsh" judgments on the earth, when in reality He has shown nothing but grace, love, and mercy while His messengers have been executed by a deceived world.

This is the answer to the prayers of the saints under the altar of the Lord who have pleaded for God's vengeance regarding their deaths. This third bowl is the answer to that prayer.

THE FOURTH BOWL: FIRE SCORCHES HUMANITY

As Christians it is our duty to stay grounded in the Word of God, the Spirit-inspired Bible, which teaches us and guides us in our decision-making. So when the Bible says that God uses the sun, moon, and stars for signs, we really need to conform our thought patterns back to the biblical perspective and not the world's view.

Genesis 1:14 reads, "Then God said, 'Let there be lights in the firmament of the heavens to divide the day from the night; and let them be for signs and seasons, and for days and years.'" The Lord uses these very real and physical celestial bodies to speak to us through signs.

Let me get this out of the way now because I know people will take this the wrong way: This is *not* astrology. We are not in any way, shape, or form guided by the stars, nor are horoscopes in any way accurate. We are simply taking the Word of God at face value—that He will use the celestial bodies at times as signs.

Not my words, His.

So when one of the bowls of judgment is massive activity from the sun, solar flares so massive and devastating that they burn people on earth, we should probably be aware of the activity of the sun.

But just think: Perhaps it is not just solar flares (although I would argue they will at least be present in this judgment). Imagine if the sun swells and grows in intensity so the entire temperature of the earth increases, not due to the carbon footprint humans leave behind but due to their sin and refusal of repentance before God.

Just imagine the pain in store for those who receive the mark of the beast. Should they still be suffering from the foul sores of the first bowl or not, either way, things are going to be beyond imagination for them. But for the sake of this hypothesis let's assume they do still have sores—how much more will it hurt to then be burned by the power of the sun?

Sunburns are some of the most painful memories I have in life, physically at least.

I have had such severe second-degree burns from them that blisters formed (they were not third-degree burns, which do not hurt as much due to the nerve endings being ruined), and I was in agony every second of the day. Nothing brought relief. Cold showers hurt because of the impact of the water. Lying down felt like torture. Even aloe vera lotions did little to soothe the heat radiating from my shoulders and back.

Don't get it twisted—the suffering and pain I experienced from severe sunburns pales in comparison to the fourth bowl of judgment. I was not in so much pain that I blasphemed God. I'll admit, I probably used language that I no longer use (we used some colorful language in the Marine Corps), but I did not curse the name of God.

> And men were scorched with great heat, and they blasphemed the name of God…and they did not repent.
>
> —REVELATION 16:9

As John records the response the followers of the beast have to their predicament after the bowl is poured out, it begs the question: Are they aware that it is God who afflicts them in such a way, or is their blasphemy of God born out of the sin-filled life they live, and they curse God's holy name regardless of what circumstances come their way? Or do the beast and false prophet blame these events on God and not on the earth's unrepentance and worship of the beast?

THE FIFTH BOWL: PAIN AND DARKNESS

There are so many possibilities in this one, and I find it entrancing to think about.

No, really! Situations like this, how darkness envelops the kingdom of the beast—I can just lie down on a couch or my bed and imagine. Of the many things that have changed about me as I've grown older, my imagination is not one of them.

How is the Lord going to send the darkness?

This is also an example of how ridiculous I find many of the arguments Christians have with each other (do not even get me started on denominations). Even when we agree over 95 percent of the things that are said and written in the Bible, we just differ on how they are implemented. Case in point, a vast majority of Christians believe in the rapture, but we will go at each other's throats about whether it is pre-tribulation, post-trib, mid-trib, etcetera.

The darkness is going to happen, folks, and we can disagree on how it may be implemented. But according to the Word of God, not my word or yours, it's going to take place.

Could darkness envelop the earth due to a total eclipse, but one that sends shock waves of fear and panic through the people because the moon and sun stand still? There is precedent for this scenario, biblical precedent, in the Book of Joshua.

In chapter 10 of the book named after him Joshua prayed to the Lord saying, "Sun, stand still over Gibeon; and Moon, in the Valley of Aijalon" (Josh. 10:12). The Bible does not tell this story as a parable, in the style of Jesus. This is not an allegory or metaphor for something else. The Word of God tells this as a literal event, and the events were said to also be recorded in "the Book of Jasher": "So the sun stood still" (Josh. 10:13).

In this time of celestial stillness, Israel's enemies, the Amorites, were slaughtered and fled from the battlefield. The bowl of darkness is similar in that the enemies of God will suffer and die, just as the enemies of Joshua did. But this time, they will have nowhere to flee.

But there is also a chance the darkness is not of solar or lunar origin.

Imagine a dark cloud similar to the one Elijah witnessed after defeating the prophets of Baal on Mount Carmel in 1 Kings 18. The darkness formed from something the size of a man's hand but continued to expand at an exponential rate, striking terror in the hearts of humanity.

Meteorologists will be dumbfounded, governments will panic, yet people will still curse the name of the Lord.

There are, of course, a wealth of other ways for the skies to darken, such as smoke from man's own pollution, which certainly would not be surprising. The darkness is said to bring with it pain, which as we've previously discussed, could be from the sores of the first bowl, or a whole new set of issues that comes with the fourth bowl.

But the pain could also be caused by smoke, mist, or a cloud that envelops the world, and within the darkness is poison. Smoke caused by pollution would certainly be a prime culprit for this, and it would be fitting that man poisons himself with his own dereliction of the duty God gave to us as the ones who hold dominion over the earth.

I'm just not convinced this is the way it will happen, however. As I see it, the angels are pouring out God's judgment, indicating to me that His wrath will bring with it something of His creation, not man's. That is certainly not to say God will not use something of man's own making to bring about His wrath. He's God. He can do what He wills in all things.

The Bowls of God's Judgment

Volcanic ash is certainly a possibility. That could definitely poison the world with the sulfur in the air. But reading the Book of Revelation, if a volcano were the source of this darkness, I feel like John would have seen this and written how he saw a mountain spew fire over the earth, darkening it in the process.

Whatever the method used to deliver this judgment, it is going to be terrible.

Imagine—you shine a flashlight outside, and it exposes nothing. You are wandering in a haze of darkness while the world likely comes to a standstill.

How could people drive in this? Have you ever driven through dense fog before? I have at night, through the Smoky Mountains in Tennessee. My wife and I were traveling from Ohio to Georgia for Christmas one year, early on in our marriage. I had my high beams on, and I could not see more than a few feet in front of my wife's Ford Escape.

When I say the fear of driving off a cliff was a reality for me, I am not kidding. I was looking down at the solid white line on my right and the dashed white lines to my left to make sure I was in the lane. I was driving around 30 miles per hour on a 65- or 70-mph freeway.

Mind you, the eighteen-wheelers were not going as slowly as I was. These truckers had way more experience driving in this kind of condition, not to mention massive lights that could probably cut through the fog.

If God sends darkness as a judgment, my best estimation is that it will make the fog I experienced in the Smoky Mountains or the fog that rolls over the Golden Gate Bridge seem like an afterthought.

This is now the second judgment John witnesses where he catalogues that the men of the world refuse to repent of their sin and again blaspheme the name of the Lord (Rev. 16:11).

Is it even possible to understand the level of spiritual oppression during this time period that will prevent people from seeing the mighty judgments of God—just as Pharaoh refused to do, but on a much larger scale—and that will fundamentally alter the earth for the remainder of its history?

By this point in the Revelation I'm thinking, "Just repent, you idiots!" But it simply will not happen. We know it will not. It cannot. It is going to happen exactly as it is written in the Word of God, and things are already in motion for these end-time events to take place.

THE SIXTH BOWL: THE RIVER EUPHRATES DRIES UP

Where do we even begin with the talk of the Tigris and Euphrates? So many historians, archaeologists, and truth-seekers have searched these rivers that have had people living off their shores for millennia.

The search for the Garden of Eden has yielded nothing, yet the river Euphrates still flows to this day. Perhaps it follows a different pattern than the days before the flood, but it still remains. It flows parallel to the Tigris to this day and goes right through the heart of modern-day Iraq.

For those of my generation, who came of age in the shadow of 9/11 and had our young adult lives dominated by the war on terror, the Euphrates River was always just a thing of legend. It was something talked about in Bible lessons, and that's it. But I've developed a strange background with the river that is to dry up and allow the armies of Armageddon to march against the nation of Israel.

> Its water was dried up, so that the way of the kings from the east might be prepared. And I saw three unclean spirits like frogs....
>
> And they gathered them together to the place called in Hebrew, Armageddon.
> —REVELATION 16:12–13, 16

The Bowls of God's Judgment

During my time in the Marine Corps, I ended up in the infantry unit of the Third Battalion, Second Marine Division as a radio operator. This unit has a storied history going back to World War II, but our history at the Battle of Nasiriyah in Iraq is what grabs my attention whenever I hear about the Euphrates River.

The city of Nasiriyah is one of many Iraqi towns on the banks of the mighty Euphrates, and it is an intriguing thing to be a part of a unit (years later, after the battle took place—I was not a combatant) with a past that fought battles where end-times events will take place.

But if the Euphrates is going to dry up in preparation for an end-times war against the nation of Israel, we need to look at what lies to the east of the Euphrates. That is the radical Islamic nation of Iran, formerly known as Persia.

Folks, there are so many verses that tell us to keep an eye on the times we live in, to compare the world we live in today to the Word of God, and to live victorious lives in Jesus Christ, regardless of the persecution we face in the process. Persecution will undoubtedly find anyone who declares the name of Jesus.

But when Iran is in the news nearly every day due to a proxy war they are engaged in with the nation of Israel, and as the world turns against God's chosen people, Christians must, must, must pay attention to the signs of the times.

On October 7, 2023, we witnessed the worst massacre the Jews have experienced since the Holocaust. The country of Iran, the spirit of Persia, celebrated this violence and continues to wish death and destruction against Israel.

The sixth bowl of judgment is a preparatory move. It is paving the way for the end-times armies to march against the nation of Israel, a literal place being prepared for a literal battle against God and His people.

We are seeing this antichrist spirit in the world today. Terror organizations like Hamas and Hezbollah attack Israel daily in these times, and the false peace of the Antichrist has not been made known in the world yet.

This spirit has been attacking the people of Israel since their inception. We see it throughout the Bible, both Old and New Testament. Satan is attacking God's people and will continue to do so until he is defeated fully at the end of time.

The Euphrates will dry up to allow armies to march across so that the day of Satan's defeat can come to fruition, all according to the Word of God.

How much more evidence does the Bible need to give to us about the spiritual warfare that the enemy commences against Israel and God's design on earth?

The three frog spirits represent this demonic attack, calling together the rest of the world against the people of God. Coming from the mouths of the dragon, the beast, and the false prophet, this shows us without question that the attacks against Israel are demonic in nature and are all a part of Satan's plan to attempt to wipe them out (v. 13).

Having this spiritual discernment about the events taking place in the Middle East today is so imperative for the church. We need to know what is truly going on behind the scenes and behind the antisemitism around the world.

Certain things taking place, such as the university protests within the United States that sparked national unrest, are clearly anti-God and anti-Israel, not pro-Palestinian as some claim. You cannot call for the eradication of an entire group of people and claim to be peaceful. But we must look at the voices we may agree with on a great many things that are also turning their backs on Israel. In America this is the America First movement.

Let me preface this by saying I love my country, the United States of America. I enlisted twice in the US military, once in the Air Force and once in the Marine Corps. I am a patriot, and *patriotism* is not a dirty word. It's a word used by those who hate this country and the Judeo-Christian values it was founded on, as they try to destroy those foundations and raise up a totalitarian, Marxist, globalist society from the ashes, with government as the replacement for God.

To this end, many have taken up the stance that we must protect America first and foremost, which in and of itself is not bad. But many prominent voices have also turned their backs on Israel, such as hate-mongering and self-described "conservative Christian" Nick Fuentes. (I rarely question a person's faith, but in this case his words and actions show he does not have Jesus living in his heart.)

This narrative that America is controlled by Israel and that Israel is evil could not be further from the truth, but it has spread like wildfire since the October 7 massacre.

Sadly, many on the conservative side of the political spectrum appear to continue down this path of abandoning Israel, such as Tucker Carlson, Candace Owens, and many more. They risk bringing about God's curse upon the nation they are fighting so hard to keep from sinking into a Marxist nightmare.

That is not to say we must agree with everything Israel does in order to support her and be an ally to the little nation in the Middle East, who is surrounded by countries that would just as soon see her destroyed.

Israel has long been a strong proponent for the LGBTQ agenda and has radical abortion access. Also, her continued ceding of territory to her enemies, territory that God gave to her, has certainly been noticed by the Lord.

But God has not abandoned her, even when He sends judgment upon His people, as He has done since ancient times. It is all in the hopes that the people will repent and turn back to Him as their one true God.

This attitude, this evil spirit and principality that is at work in the world today, will be around during these times as well. It is what keeps people from repenting throughout the judgments and keeps the satanic hatred of Israel alive and well.

That is why I can never support a movement, even one for a country I love such as the United States, when they are turning their back on the nation of Israel.

As I have said, but it needs repeating from now until Jesus returns in His full glory, the Abrahamic covenant is alive and well today. There is nothing, not an iota of evidence, to say otherwise. While Jesus is the fulfillment of the Law (not the destroyer of it) and bridges the gap between us and His Father, He very much loves the nation of Israel. This is evident in His words found within the Holy Bible.

That is why in the end of times, as the Euphrates River is dried up for satanic armies to march across and attack God's chosen people in the country of Israel (perhaps even in all of the land God promised to her), there will be those who hate this chosen nation with a supernatural fervor.

JESUS SPEAKS

How amazing is this for John? During this part of the vision, as he is witnessing God's judgment upon the earth, he hears his Savior's voice ring out with power and authority before the final bowl, saying,

> Behold, I am coming as a thief. Blessed is he who watches, and keeps his garments, lest he walk naked and they see his shame.
> —REVELATION 16:15

How many times must we be told to watch? "Blessed is he who watches." I want the Lord's blessing, don't you?

Jesus is once again proclaiming that He is coming, quickly and when it is not expected, and those who are prepared will go with Him.

Those who are not are *naked*, as He says. As the old saying goes, they are "caught with their pants down," which I feel is fitting here. Jesus Himself says all will see the shame of those who are left behind.

Discernment of the times is so important. How do I know that? Because the Bible keeps telling us this over and over and over again.

These are not my words to try to scare you; it is God's Word trying to get us to prepare our hearts and tell as many people as we can about the truth of Jesus Christ so that they are not left behind to suffer in eternity, separated from their Creator in a pit of fire and torment.

You do not have to believe that the seals on the scroll, the trumpets, or the bowl judgments will be revealed in a literal fashion the way I do, but I would strongly encourage you heed the words of Jesus Christ when it comes to being prepared for His literal return.

Considering the atmosphere that this part of the Revelation is written in, we can even read Jesus' almost unexpected words to John as a warning.

The world is burning and in the throes of judgment. Meanwhile, the very next verse after the words of Jesus is about the mobilization of forces against the Lamb and His army. It's almost like He is giving them one last chance, saying, "I'm coming. Y'all better get ready, because it's going to happen, and if you are not on My side, you are going to have a bad time of it."

We know the kings of the world will not repent and join the Lamb, to their own destruction.

THE SEVENTH BOWL: THE GREAT EARTHQUAKE AND HAILSTORM

John often describes events in the Revelation with the power level they bring with them. In this case it is no small voice that rings out from the throne of heaven, in the tabernacle, which the smoke of the Lord filled (Rev. 15:8). It was so great no one could tolerate being in His presence, as it was in Solomon's temple as well.

It was the Lord who gave the order to pour out His judgment, and it is my firm belief that it is the Lord God Almighty who gives the final say, "It is done!" (Rev. 16:17), similar to the last words of Jesus at His crucifixion: "It is finished!" (John 19:30).

With His words the end of the earth as it is known begins.

The great earthquake, the likes of which we have never seen before, brings another interesting possibility: the literal moving of mountains and islands that God may have also moved during the flood or the time of the Tower of Babel when He scattered humanity. Will this cataclysmic event bring a coalescing of land back together as He had originally created it?

Another striking feature John is witnessing is the utter hardheartedness of the people of earth throughout these ordeals. They are so spiritually oppressed and deceived, so stubbornly opposed to God, their Creator, that they refuse over and over again to repent and will suffer a fate much worse than the hardhearted Egyptians of Moses' day.

As the powerful voice declares the final bowl judgment, the greatest earthquake in human history strikes, an apocalyptic event that shakes the earth to its core, setting the stage for the very end.

John witnesses the fall of Babylon, a principality, which is no small event (Rev. 16:19). Babylon is more than just a once-great empire. At the time of John, many also associated Babylon with Rome, the then-current world power. But it also represents every major world power.

How could this be? Because every single empire has fallen, and all it takes is a look back through history to see the evil that contributes to the fall of a nation, even God's chosen people of Israel.

As an American it is easy for me to see how our founding was unique, based upon the Judeo-Christian principles found in the Bible. But over the decades, we have fallen away from these values and replaced them with the pagan and satanic practices that saw Israel fall in ancient times.

We murder our babies, celebrate sexual immorality on a scale that is inconceivable, allow corruption to rule the halls of Congress—the list is far too long to write here. But understand this: America is deserving of the judgment she is facing.

We have failed to repent as a nation for our sin, which is deserving of death. And having been founded as a nation that honors God, the United States can expect a great fall from grace.

It is this stubbornness and embracing of sin, of man's ways, that has led to John witnessing this great earthquake and hailstorm that causes humanity to blaspheme the Lord.

If only they would heed the words in the Holy Bible and repent of this wickedness and cast the devil out from their midst. But, according to the Word of God, this will not happen. That is not to say Christians should not work to fulfill the Great Commission every day of our lives so that as many as possible will accept the saving knowledge of Jesus Christ.

Do we think this is what God wanted? That destroying the world He created for fellowship with man was His intent? No! We brought this and the curse of sin upon ourselves. Adam and Eve could have resisted the serpent; they could have heeded the warning of the Lord. As our progenitors, we are guilty right beside them.

But because we have aligned ourselves with spirits like that of Babylon, for the perfect kingdom of God to reign for eternity, things must be done away with.

Nations must fall, and the world infected with sin must go away.

CHAPTER 17

The SCARLET HARLOT

By this point if I were John, I would have to wonder just how much more of the end-times God has in store for me. John has now witnessed the judgment of the earth for humanity's sin, but as the late-night infomercial hosts used to say, "We're not done yet."

The next three chapters discuss the fall of one of the most destructive principalities in hell's army: Babylon.

While there was, of course, a historical nation of Babylon, this spirit represented by a woman, a harlot, is the force behind the lust aspect of the flesh. She, Babylon, has been at war against the sexuality and gender God designed from the very beginning. Think of her as being a member of Satan's Joint Chiefs of Staff.

From the pagan ancient times, she was present with prostitutes roaming the halls of false gods. As the gospel spread throughout history, men and women still fell to her seduction and committed acts unbecoming of God's creation.

Her influence is alive and thriving today in all forms of sexual immorality and the abandonment of God's design for gender in cultures worldwide.

Whenever the name *Lilith* has come up in society, usually associated with rebellion, radical feminism, and a false sense of freedom (which is really spiritual oppression), Babylon is at work.

Whenever pornography became accepted and warped the minds of both the young and the old and reduced the sanctity and holiness of the act, Babylon was there.

Whenever men of great importance, such as Kings David and

Solomon, allowed themselves to be tempted by the flesh and then fell to that temptation, Babylon was behind the scheme.

Throughout all human history, in every culture, the lust of the flesh has consumed rulers of the earth: money, fame, power, sexual desires—all these things and more have led the leadership of the world astray, and they have sinned before the Lord.

John is now shown Mystery Babylon, who is responsible for wars fought in her name, billions who have suffered due to her greed and perversion, and countless seduced away from God, their Creator, because of her (Rev. 17:3–6).

Not even the church has been spared her influence and pull.

How many times has the body of Christ embarrassed our Savior with high-profile personalities, broadcast around the world, falling to the pulls of the flesh?

Sadly, whenever I read these verses about Babylon and her influence, I always think of the televangelist scandals, specifically of the late 1980s.

The stain they caused remains to this day; I was barely a child when they came to light. I also know there has been repentance from some of those who fell in front of the whole world. This is not an attempt to shame them but instead to learn from their tales and instill a deep cornerstone in future generations.

No denomination has been spared from the allure and seduction of this Mystery Babylon. John is about to witness her finally reaping the rewards of the blood she has shed over the millennia. Now John is whisked away in the Spirit to witness her fate.

It must be noted how important God must find this series of events to be. We are reading about the final moments of the cause behind so much of the hurt and defilement in the world today.

Read through the entire Bible, both Old and New Testament, and see just how many references there are to God's abhorrence of sexual immorality. He loathes it. He detests it, and this ruler of darkness, Babylon, has been seducing mankind to perform abominable acts against the Lord from the beginning.

Do not forget sexual immorality was one of the driving factors for God flooding the earth in the first place.

For all the adornments John sees the mother of harlots and prostitutes in, it cannot hide her ugliness. She is not to be looked upon as a thing of beauty because she is a deceiver, wrapped in fine cloth and jewels to trick the kings of history into lying in bed with her and defiling their rule and kingdoms.

Yet the visage of her must have been a striking sight to behold atop the scarlet beast, for even John marvels at her, perhaps due to how great her evil truly is and the effect that it has on her image.

> I saw a woman sitting on a scarlet beast which was full of names of blasphemy, having seven heads and ten horns....
>
> I saw the woman, drunk with the blood of the saints and with the blood of the martyrs....I marveled with great amazement.
> —Revelation 17:3, 6

The elite class and its perversion are not new, but as time has unfolded and society has rejected God while embracing the harlot and drinking from her cup, depravity has surpassed even the time of Noah. Babylon has corrupted the very design of the humanity God has created, and no amount of earthly fulfillment can compare to the glory of God and being in His presence.

This love of the world, including religiosity and legalism, led to the deaths of many saints. As we've already said and will continue to say since it is important for Christians to understand, Jesus told His disciples, "If the world hates you, you know that it hated Me before it hated you" (John 15:18). This is in part due to the harlot Babylon being unable to tolerate that which is righteous and good and getting drunk on the blood of Jesus' saints. She revels in it, rejoicing in unholy glee at the sight of men like Stephen who are killed for proclaiming the name of Jesus.

This joy in destroying that which is God's is a false joy in and of itself, for the Lord's saints are shut up under the altar of God until their time is over. Nothing of God's is destroyed by her, simply corrupted, because the church is still very much alive and well.

So here's a little branching theory that I have, which is the point of this book: to talk about the Book of Revelation and its possible meanings. Anyone who says they've got it completely figured out doesn't.

THE HARLOT IS DESTROYED

The harlot sits atop seven mountains that could represent spiritual principalities under her command and influence (Rev. 17:9), as she is the progenitor of abomination. Do not confuse these words: From Lucifer came sin, and other evil rulers hold authority over specific regions and actions. Think of mammon, the worship of money and greed above God. That is a principality.

There are also regional spirits. Take the prince of Persia who fought angels in the Book of Daniel. These nations could be ruled over by the principalities, and it could be reflective of their cultures—groups of peoples given to ways God finds abominable and detests. Frankly, we can see societies around the world turning to these ways today.

Meanwhile, the ten kings are not as of yet; they are to come: "The ten horns which you saw are ten kings who have received no kingdom as yet, but they receive authority for one hour as kings with the beast" (v. 12). These could be the rulers of the day when the beast takes control over the world, so perhaps people should keep their eyes open for a ten-seat or ten-nation alliance in the future. They would be the ones to hand the world's power over to the beast and usher in the tribulation.

This would be how he gains power over God's creation, at least on the surface. We know that God is ultimately in control, and it is a part of His plan for the beast to temporarily rise into power and deceive humanity, just as Satan did in the Garden of Eden.

Yet even as God has ordained this event to occur, something must happen between the beast and the harlot for him to have his ten kings destroy her, perhaps in a form of consolidating his power and having no rivals against him.

Being considered a rival to the beast would equate to massive amounts of power for Babylon and her ability to influence, corrupt, and destroy.

Her power is evident as John witnesses her symbolic drinking of the blood of the martyrs that has been spilled. She revels in this, just as the witch-queen Jezebel did, who could be considered an operative of Babylon. Everything Jezebel represents Babylon represents and more.

It's actually crazy when you dig deep into this relatively short chapter that reveals so much of what the end-times are going to be like.

The Bible says that as the harlot is destroyed by the beast and his followers, it is God's purpose during these times that those still on the earth will "be of one mind" when they hand power over to the beast (v. 17, MEV).

To me this says clearly that the church will not be present during such times because those who believe in Jesus Christ will not be of one mind with those who give their kingdom—the earth—over to the beast.

Now, there can be an argument that this is instead a specific kingdom and not the entire world. I really do not want to be dismissive toward those who believe in the post-tribulation rapture; I simply do not see how the Bible teaches remnant kingdoms will be in existence when the beast comes into power.

In fact, I believe it teaches the opposite.

From what we gain from the Scriptures there will be one nation that will be in good standing with the Lord during the end-times, and that will be the nation of Israel.

There may be "neutral" nations as far as their impact on global politics, power, and commerce. (I'm not being demeaning, but I greatly doubt that the nations of Mongolia, Lithuania, and New Zealand will be major powers during these times.) However, there will be a global system in place for the mark of the beast to be established and implemented upon all cultures of the world.

On top of this these nations and their rulers have also drunk from the cup of Babylon, have given in to her seduction, and will pay the price for it—the same as she will pay the price for her perverse deception and slaying of the saints.

CHAPTER 18

The WORLD MOURNS as BABYLON FALLS

JOHN AGAIN WITNESSES a mighty angel descend from heaven, a common event throughout Revelation, and he references the angel having his own glory (Rev. 18:1). Could this have been the case for Lucifer as well, except for the fact that he believed the glory given to him by God could actually rival his Maker's?

Imagine this great angel witnessing the Lord dispatch another angelic being greater than he. Would a lesson be learned, or would his faith and obedience to God be strengthened even more?

The angel has to be of very high status within the heavenlies, as John knows he has great authority. It's not every day that an angel's glory illuminates the entire world. This is an event we would likely attribute to Jesus, but in this case it is an angel.

Glory like this is appropriate for the situation, considering he is announcing the fall of Babylon, one of the most significant events in the history of the Lord's creation.

Why? Because this is the fall of one of the greatest principalities in history. This is the great seductress meeting her end. This is a great fulfillment of biblical prophecy and a sure sign of the soon return of Jesus Christ. It is so important that it warrants an entire chapter in one of the most consequential books in the Bible, which is the Word of God.

As John hears and sees the declaration that the mystery that is Babylon is defeated and done away with—at the hands of the beast and his kings, no less—the world will mourn.

Do we not see this in our society today, this enchantment

the devil and his forces have over people so that they weep when evil and evildoers are thwarted or die in some fashion?

In the United States, and it pains me to say this, there are those who mourn when restrictions on abortion are put into place.[1] They are deceived into worshipping death, cry out when evil is replaced with goodness, and rejoice when good is thwarted for unrighteousness.

The leaders who for millennia yielded to Babylon's perversions and seductions—the elite and wealthy who sold their souls for earthly glory, fame, and riches—will lose it all. A spiritual dam will break at her demise as the grip she held over the earth will at last be broken. Even as her demise takes shape, the world will be cursed by it one last time as death, mourning, and famine will take her place.

This could take place in any number of ways. People could kill each other in the streets at the demise of Babylon. Trade routes and commerce could shut down, leading to empty stores and, in turn, riots as people turn on one another for supplies.

We've seen it before, and you can bet we will see it again, but on a much larger and harsher scale. As described by John, with all the wealth accumulated in the service of Babylon evaporating, a worldwide economic collapse is likely to happen (vv. 11–18).

> The merchants of the earth will weep and mourn over her, for no one buys their merchandise any more.
> —REVELATION 18:11, MEV

OK, time for random theory time again. The end of the merchants' items that they sell shows a potential evil that has returned to the earth: mass enslavement.

For merchants may sell the bodies and souls of men—perhaps as slaves, perhaps as prostitutes.

The men of the world in these times may be willing to sell

their souls, as they do today, in the hopes of gaining their riches back, for fame or power.

Abandoning any semblance of morals or principles, faith, and priorities, they will act as though their souls are drunk from the wine of Babylon, forgetting who they are and who created them, abandoning their humanity.

This is how great the enemy's deception and influence truly is.

Now, back to theory time—for discussion's sake! As John is listening to the various voices decreeing the downfall of Babylon, we know this is a principality, but the wording and imagery used also point to the pinnacle of Babylon being destroyed—a great city reminiscent of Rome during ancient times: "Alas, alas, that great city" (vv. 16, 19).

Could there be a modern-day equivalent of Rome in the world when God renders judgment upon Babylon? When the principality is destroyed, will her stronghold in the world also collapse in on itself?

In particular, as the mighty angel throws the millstone into the sea, signifying the total and complete destruction of Babylon, John is being told that the great city known as Babylon will be thrown down "with violence" (v. 21).

Now, this can mean any number of things. Again, this is theory time, thinking time. What could it mean? Perhaps an invading force of some kind, either domestic or international, invades this city?

The first thing that comes to my mind when I read this, and I do not say this to be bombastic or dramatic, is a nuclear strike hitting a city. We have not seen the use of nuclear or atomic weapons since the bombings of Hiroshima and Nagasaki to end World War II, the greatest war ever fought so far.

As John recites the finality of Babylon's demise, we have already gone over the economic impact that he writes about, but this comes with a disruption of entertainment as well.

John tells us that the music in Babylon, which I firmly

believe will also be a literal city, will stop. The world will mourn the end of Babylon, and with her death comes the end of her influence.

The music that she emitted will be silenced. This includes all mediums that broadcast the "harpists, musicians, flutists, and trumpeters" found throughout the entertainment spectrum, from concerts to movies and television (v. 22).

All these things—the music from the city, the commerce, and most notably (to me) the violence of Babylon—will cease, and while the world mourns these events, heaven rejoices.

Ending this chapter on Babylon's demise, John writes something that catches my eye (and I'm sure that of many who have read the verses), which I fear many Christians simply do not put much effort into understanding anymore.

That is the wording John uses to describe how Babylon deceived the nations: her "sorcery" (v. 23).

I fear we do not address sorcery or witchcraft nearly as much as we need to in the church. Many simply view it as a thing of the past, not seeing it as the spiritual snare and danger that it really is.

As I've said before and will say again, do not take my word for it; take God at His Word.

Here is a brief list of books, chapters, and verses that address sorcery and witchcraft:

- Exodus 22:18
- Leviticus 19:31; 20:6, 27
- Isaiah 8:19
- Ezekiel 13:6–9

"But James, you clod, you heretic, those are all verses in the Old Testament, and I'm a New Covenant Christian!"

Well, buckle up because Paul and others expressly address these issues as well, and the abominations that they truly are:

- Acts 16:16–18; 19:19
- Galatians 5:19–21
- Revelation 9:21 (as we've previously covered)

This is by no means an exhaustive list, just a quick reference to prove the point I am trying to make: Sorcery, demonic magic, is real and dangerous. It is so dangerous, in fact, that the Bible talks about it in both the Old and New Testaments again and again.

But the devil, not just Babylon, is very good at disguising it and making it appear "sexy" or "no big deal." They have the capability to desensitize humanity to sorcery, witchcraft, and the occult, things that would not happen to a biblically sound and discerning society.

This shows us a clear picture that many cultures have abandoned these godly principles and have succumbed to the allure of seduction and sorcery. This description by John shows that sorcery, divination (tarot cards and astrology), and witchcraft are still alive and well when Babylon is destroyed.

These things seduce people into the ways of the world through the practice of "manifesting" riches, fame, and success. Don't believe me? Just check out TikTok, and you will see a world alive and brimming with this type of sorcery. It has made a roaring comeback into society because the church, well, the church has failed in America, in my opinion.

There is, of course, and always will be a remnant of churches that abide by biblical ways. I know of many, and they are Spirit-filled believers making an impact in their communities and beyond.

But that does not make up for the millions of lukewarm Christians who have sat idly by and allowed corruption, seduction, and false teachings to infiltrate their ranks and cause their churches not only to be ineffective at shaping the culture but instead to succumb to it.

That is the sorcery of Babylon, who has tempted church leaders, kings and queens, and titans of business into her web of earthly promises that ultimately lead to a life of eternal death and separation from God, their Creator.

Far too many in today's society and churches, much less in the days to come, have made the conscious decision to try to please man instead of God. The goal is to get butts in the seats and give a feel-good message that does not offend anyone.

I hate to break it to you if you are preaching this type of message, but you are doing yourself and your congregation a disservice by not speaking the Word of God in full.

There are difficult parts to read, especially in the Revelation given to John! But each and every word of the Bible was deemed important enough by God Himself to have it included for either one reason or many.

To select certain passages and not teach on them or on the warnings God gives us about very real and serious issues in life is ultimately doing God a disservice and leading people away from His full message in His holy Word.

That is not something I would want to answer for on judgment day.

CHAPTER 19

HEAVEN REJOICES

I**F YOU ARE** not aware, vengeance is not ours to take while on earth. Our flesh craves it, demands it, when someone hurts, offends, or upsets us. I am among the guiltiest of those whose flesh cries out to hurt those who seek to hurt me or my family. Allow me to clarify I am not talking about self-defense for self-preservation; I fully support this. I am talking about acting as the judge and jury instead of allowing God to fulfill this role.

> Vengeance is Mine, and recompense; their foot shall slip in due time; for the day of their calamity is at hand, and the things to come hasten upon them.
> —Deuteronomy 32:35

> Beloved, do not avenge yourselves, but rather give place to wrath; for it is written, "Vengeance is Mine, I will repay," says the Lord.
> —Romans 12:19

> For we know Him who said, "Vengeance is Mine, I will repay," says the Lord. And again, "The Lord will judge His people."
> —Hebrews 10:30

It is a tough thing to do, submitting ourselves to His commands, but as we see in chapter 19, God's vengeance is coming, and it is going to be on a scale we simply cannot fathom at the moment. But when it comes, all heaven will rejoice in His fulfilled prophecy.

John hears this symphony in heaven, glorifying the Lord at Babylon's end.

Could these voices, this great multitude, be the souls who met their demise at Babylon's hand? Are they the souls who inhabit the space under the altar of God in heaven, souls whose blood she drank to the point of drunkenness?

I do believe this symbolism of her drinking the saints' blood is metaphorical, but I also firmly believe that Babylon took great joy, pleasure, and empowerment from the spiritual darkness that overtook many who killed the followers of Jesus, as well as the Jewish people killed for their heritage.

Were Babylon's victims so numerous, spanning the ages, that when they rejoice, it creates such a great noise in heaven that the elders, creatures of the throne room, and angelic hosts join in the praise being lifted up to the Lord for this momentous occasion in which His vengeance is finally dealt out?

As we can see throughout the entirety of the Bible, God's judgment is declared true and righteous, from the trumpets' call for repentance to the wrath of the bowls and Babylon's horrific demise. He is justified in these acts, which counter affronts to His perfect ways.

The corruption of sin must, and will, be burned out.

This encounter in heaven, the rejoicing and praise of the Lord for Babylon's demise, really makes you think back to the Old Testament victories of Israel on the physical battlefield.

What proceeded from the mouths of the Israelites after victories in battle when they were led by the likes of Joshua and David? Praise! Joshua renewed the covenant between Israel and the Lord, while David is well known for his praise of the Lord Most High.

Praise, worship, and adoration were poured out to Adonai for victory over the enemy, and that has not changed as Mystery Babylon meets her end and all heaven rejoices, giving God the praise and honor He is due.

> And I heard, as it were, the voice of a great multitude, as the sound of many waters and as the sound of mighty thunderings, saying, "Alleluia!...Let us be glad and rejoice and give Him glory, for the marriage of the Lamb has come."...
>
> Then he said to me, "Write: 'Blessed are those who are called to the marriage supper of the Lamb!'"... And I fell at his feet to worship him. But he said to me, "See that you do not do that!
>
> —REVELATION 19:6–7, 9–10

The angel of the Lord, which John witnesses, understands the seriousness of glorifying the Lord and offering only Him praise and glory. With this understanding he must correct John, for even the apostle given the Revelation misunderstands the words the angel says, and John asserts a godhood position on the messenger; he must be rebuked for his actions.

Now, I did a little deeper looking into chapter 19, in the Greek to be specific, because I wanted to see if the word *angelos* was anywhere in the chapter (Blue Letter Bible for the win).

It does not appear, and the chapter only refers to *he*, whom John is talking to.

In the previous chapter John refers to two angels that he sees: one who cries out that Babylon has fallen and another who throws the millstone into the sea and has a saying to go along with that.

Separate from these encounters in chapter 18 is a voice proclaimed from heaven—not identified as an angel, elder, creature, God Himself, or any other potential speaker—just a loud and mighty voice.

So when we get to John's encounter with the angelic being in chapter 19, the being says things that to me—and I can only speak for myself—are the words of not an angel but instead a human who has been sanctified in heaven with a new body.

Let's look at what he says in verse 10:

> See that you do not do that! I am your fellow servant, and of your brethren who have the testimony of Jesus. Worship God! For the testimony of Jesus is the spirit of prophecy.
> —REVELATION 19:10

There's that word again, *prophecy*. But perhaps that's for another book at another time. Now, let's see what the English Standard Version has to say:

> You must not do that! I am a fellow servant with you and your brothers who hold to the testimony of Jesus. Worship God.
> —REVELATION 19:10, ESV

We see some delineations here, don't we? The quote ends before the statement of prophecy, and the words of the person imply shared servitude but a distinct separation from "you and your brothers," in which he does not appear to include himself.

OK, so let's go with the Amplified Bible since the third time's the charm and Jesus rose on the third day:

> You must not do that; I am a fellow servant with you and your brothers and sisters who have and hold the testimony of Jesus. Worship God [alone]. For the testimony of Jesus is the spirit of prophecy [His life and teaching are the heart of prophecy].
> —REVELATION 19:10, AMP

Well, well, well, the plot thickens.

The speaker and John are still not quite unified in their shared origin, but we see a stronger connection than what the ESV appears to profess. Without mentioning the inclusion of sisters in the faith, which is beside the point, the message remains the same: Worship God and Him alone, and Jesus (who is the Word) is also at the very heart of prophecy.

Understand that I am a dreamer. I may be getting older each day (but I'm still not *old* old), but my imagination is as strong as ever.

These words just stand apart to me from how we see angelic beings—messengers and warriors—talk in other verses. I say this as a wonder, but perhaps if we follow the implication, then this is one of the disciples who was with John but has been granted a new body and a new charge at the end of days.

It makes sense to me that Jesus would still utilize His disciples. Those who followed Him to the death in life would also have a role to play when they are made perfect in the end-times.

Just a thought. But this just shows how much there is in the Book of Revelation and, to me, how mightily interesting it is and how important it is to discuss Scripture and deepen our understanding of it together!

I suppose it has to be said, or I may stand accused, that we are not to come up with wild theories that do not align with Scripture. Anything—any word, thought, or idea—that deviates from Scripture is not of God and must be cast aside immediately.

God does not contradict Himself, and if the Bible is His inerrant Word, then any theories that run counter to it are not of Him but instead are deceptive in nature. And we know who the father of lies is, don't we?

THE RIDER ON THE WHITE HORSE

There are no words in the human language to fully encapsulate the greatness of the appearance of Jesus, fully ready to go to war for His kingdom.

> Behold, a white horse. And He who sat on him was called Faithful and True, and in righteousness He judges and makes war. His eyes were like a flame of fire, and on His head were many crowns. He

had a name written that no one knew except Himself. He was clothed with a robe dipped in blood, and His name is called The Word of God.
—REVELATION 19:11–13

His intentions and actions of judgment and making war against sin itself are as justified and righteous as God's judgment of the earth and its inhabitants.

He earned this justification over sin and death through His sinless death and subsequent resurrection. By the shedding of His innocent and sacrificial blood on the cross, He established His victory over the grave three days later when He walked out of the tomb.

John witnesses this amazing event. I mean, can you picture the most raucous sports arena you can imagine going absolutely ballistic for their team? What comes to my mind is a European soccer match; those crowds go wild. (Yes, yes, I know South American crowds are said to be just as energetic, but I have not had the pleasure of watching as many highlights of their matches on YouTube as I have European games, so please pardon my ignorance.)

If you were enjoying a Spirit-filled Christian church in the 1990s like I was, you probably heard the song "We Will Ride." From what I have gathered, this was written by none other than Lindell Cooley, most notably known as the worship leader of the Brownsville Revival.

That is what comes to my mind when reading of the great entrance of Jesus Christ, Warrior-King.

And this is what all the evil that we are enduring, the spiritual darkness and oppression, is leading up to: the return of Jesus Christ.

It is so easy for us to get overwhelmed by the growing evil in the world and what appears to be the diminished effect of the gospel in society. But nothing could be further from the truth!

THE REVELATION OF JESUS

Satan wants us to think that the Bible is irrelevant, that the power and wisdom of God are not found in the pages of His Word. And sadly, many have bought into this lie!

But as John witnesses Jesus' triumphant return, we see that Satan's plan ultimately fails, and the world—all the humanity that ever is or was or will be—will see the truth found in the Word, which is Jesus.

As usual, as we read this immense event, apocalyptic in nature, I find myself wondering: Well, what's this hidden name that Jesus has?

We already know many of the names of Jesus, but this one is a mystery. The way that John writes it, or that it is translated, is mysterious as well, as the tone suggests that at the time of Jesus' return, still no one knows the name.

Perhaps it is something that will be revealed later, at the end of times as He claims His kingship as Lord over the new heaven and new earth?

It still bewilders me, in a wondrous way, that He does in fact have His title of "King of kings, and Lord of lords" essentially tattooed (written or inscribed) on His leg (v. 16). While I know some people hold very strong feelings toward tattoos, both for and against, this does not sway me one way or another, as it is (1) a part of a vision and could be symbolic, and (2) simply not a topic worth arguing over, in my opinion. Some people, both Christians and not, are not convicted about tattoos.

Tattoos and markings fall under the Levitical Law, which by and large Christians do not live under to the letter but instead use as an outline for godly living. If this were not true, then people living a homosexual lifestyle would be put to death, according to Leviticus 20:13, and the only place that is happening is not in Christian or Jewish nations but in Islamic nations, regions, and territories.

I got a couple of tattoos when I was younger, both before I turned twenty-one, and I do not feel convicted about having either one. They both have to do with my Christian faith (I know there are many fellow believers who have received much more explicit tattoos in their lives). But on that same note I do not plan on getting any more, as there are both practical and personal reasons for me not wanting to put more ink on my skin.

But I certainly do not believe this is an area that deserves condemnation and calls for repentance simply because you've got some ink. The church has a bad enough reputation of being a bunch of finger-pointing hypocrites, instead of the grace-giving disciples of Jesus.

Regardless, it is just as feasible that this is a symbolic image, of which there are many throughout the Bible. Jesus did observe the Law, and fulfilled it, during His lifetime. And according to the words given to Moses, it was against the Lord's desire to see His people (Israel) with tattoos. And since the Son and the Father are one, Jesus would not go against the wishes of the Father.

While the writing and descriptions of Jesus' triumphant return with an army at His back take up much of a reader's attention (I mean, let's be honest, this is the return we are all waiting for), they also show us the defeat of the beast and the false prophet (Rev. 19:19–21).

There is no mercy for those who stand with the beast. The time for repentance has passed, and now the evil ones find themselves standing in the way of Jesus establishing His kingdom according to the will of the Father.

The slaughter of the kings and armies of the earth is a complete and total victory for Jesus and His army dressed in white. The power structure of Satan's plans is torn down, with the beast and the false prophet being taken into custody by the forces of the Lamb and cast into the eternal lake of fire and brimstone.

A fate far worse than anything our mortal minds can comprehend.

CHAPTER 20

The END of TIME

THINGS ARE REALLY getting down to the wire in the Revelation given to John now. The great tribulation is over, and as John describes the angel coming down from heaven, the implication appears that his place of vision has shifted to a spiritual view of the earth.

> Then I saw an angel coming down from heaven....He laid hold of the dragon...and he cast him into the bottomless pit, and shut him up, and set a seal on him, so that he should deceive the nations no more till the thousand years were finished.
> —REVELATION 20:1–3

Isn't it interesting? John sees an angel granted power and authority to bind and cast out the devil from earth into the bottomless pit, setting a seal upon him that cannot be broken until a set time, much like the scrolls to the end-of-time churches. And with this seal comes a golden age on the earth for a thousand years under Jesus' rule.

But according to God's plan, and to much of humanity's dismay, the devil, who is Satan, will once again be given reign to torment and deceive the earth before his final defeat.

And in these upcoming verses stands a pillar as to why many believe that the rapture is in fact going to take place after the great tribulation, and who could blame them? This is when John witnesses what he refers to as the "first resurrection" (v. 6).

Some believe the rapture and the first resurrection are two separate events, while others believe that they are the same.

Since pre- and post-tribulation rapture beliefs are the two prominent systems of belief, that is why I am mainly addressing only these two—not to insult those who believe in the variety of other systems concerning who, what, where, and when Jesus returns for His church.

The way I see it, this should not be the divisive point of contention that it has become within the church. Neither view is heretical, nor are the others, because the primary points of salvation and faith are still the same. It is literally a difference of opinion on when Jesus raptures His church, not if.

Oh, how wonderful the bonds between the various churches would be if we as Christians focused on what unites us in Christ instead of how our theologies differ. We bicker back and forth on topics, just like Jesus' disciples did during their years of evangelism with Him, and we see that through His constant correcting of their thinking.

Catholics versus Protestants. Cessationists versus continuationists. (If you are not familiar with this split, these are [respectively] those who believe the giftings of the Holy Spirit ended after the apostolic age and those who believe they are still bestowed upon believers today.) Pre-tribbers versus post-tribbers. Denomination versus denomination versus denomination.

All this division will melt away the moment we see our King. If only we would stop it of our own accord while here on earth. We may just make a far greater difference in society than what is being made today and save a few more lives along the way as well.

Regardless of the individual or group beliefs of the order of events, John does stand and witness what he calls the first resurrection, or the resurrection of the saints: those who were killed for the gospel, those who maintained the faith during the great tribulation (no small task to be sure!), and those who rejected the beast and his false prophet, along with their lies (v. 4). Imagine the severe social and cultural persecution this group of saints will have to endure!

We've already seen the very tip of the cancel culture iceberg,[1] and you can guarantee the system in place during the beast's reign will be much, much worse. But this level of cancel culture under the beast will just be persecution under a different name.

Jail. Inability to buy and sell. Beatings. We see this in our world today, on different levels and by different means depending on the country you go to.

But should the beast's system in fact be Islam—well, just look at Sharia law and its punishments. That is what we can expect to see to the very extreme.

But those who refuse to bend the knee before this oppressive and evil regime will reign with Christ in glory during the millennial rule.

The Millennium

Now, whether this reign that John sees with them under the rulership of Jesus is a literal thousand years remains to be seen. We have seen periods of time used as metaphors in other places in the Bible—case in point, the mysterious weeks and their timeline from the Book of Daniel.

Whether this is a thousand years by human standards or if it is a measure of time determined by God described as a thousand years will only become known for certain when Jesus does in fact return.

This is another part of the Bible that my imagination just runs wild with. Can you imagine such a period of time (I often think of the years AD 1000 to AD 2000 and all that took place within that time frame) and imagine that long of a reign with Jesus Christ? The earth would be totally different from what we see today after the bowls of judgment are poured out onto the earth.

What kinds of systems would be set up? Would there be currencies? Would we just be able to live during this millennial reign instead of work the way we do today?

Will it be like life in Eden before Adam and Eve condemned us to a life of toil in a sin-cursed world?

Those who reign with Christ for a thousand years seem to have specific attributes mentioned in Revelation 20:4:

- They were beheaded (killed) for their witness of Jesus and the Word of God.
- They had not worshipped the beast or his image (during the great tribulation).
- They had not received the mark of the beast during the beast's reign.

What awaits those not resurrected with Jesus for His millennial reign? Will those who have not declared Him as Lord be given a chance at repentance? Doubtful. Or will they have any concept of time while in a sleep, slumber, or purgatory of some kind?

Regardless, when all awaken for the second resurrection, their final judgment awaits before the Lord of lords.

As we read what John writes further into the Revelation, during the "great white throne" judgment all the dead are resurrected in the second resurrection (vv. 11–12). The way he writes this, to me, implies that there will be those who are raised in this event whose names are going to be found in the Book of Life.

Why? Because he specifically distinguishes what happens to those who are not found in the Book of Life and the second death that they will encounter in the lake of fire along with Satan, the beast, and the false prophet.

Look at verse 15 specifically: "Anyone not found written in the Book of Life was cast into the lake of fire."

By mentioning that there are those who are not written in the Lamb's Book of Life, it implies to me that there are, in fact, those whose names are written in the Book of Life during the second resurrection, or else would he not have written that all those raised in the event were cast into the fire?

But backing up a few verses, the world Jesus will reign over for a thousand years will not be perfect, mind you. Even though Jesus is in power and Satan is locked up during this time in the bottomless pit, not the lake of fire, he will again be released to terrorize the earth for a short period of time.

Many have pondered the reasoning God has for this brief period of time before the great white throne judgment.

I can think of few verses in the Bible that exemplify the message of Isaiah 55:8–9, which reads:

> "For My thoughts are not your thoughts, nor are your ways My ways," says the LORD. "For as the heavens are higher than the earth, so are My ways higher than your ways, and My thoughts than your thoughts."

Why on earth would God allow Satan to terrorize and deceive the nations again? And Satan is going to mobilize Gog and Magog along with a grand army to war against Jesus (Rev. 20:7–8).

No human will ever know the full reasoning for this, but there are some possible answers why. This could be the setup for his ultimate defeat in front of the entire world right at the end of history. Because after these events and after Satan is cast into the lake of fire—or hell as we call it—the creation period of time comes to an end.

There is no escape for Lucifer, the beast, and the false prophet after this time. Their reign of terror comes to an end, and they will soon be joined by "Death and Hades" (v. 14, MEV). Sin is no more, and God's creation—well, the ones who accepted Jesus as their Lord and Savior, at least—will be able to live a life with God as He meant for it to be.

THE GREAT WHITE THRONE JUDGMENT

The end of the old has finally come and paves the way for the new heaven and the new earth. History has reached its end.

Perhaps new history is being written, as John sees multiple books open during this final judgment, but they are most likely the books detailing the lives of those facing the judgment of King Jesus, as John describes the dead as being judged according to their deeds—which include whether they proclaimed the name of Jesus during their lifetimes (v. 12).

But only one of those books is the Lamb's Book of Life. To die spiritually and be separated from God is the true and torturous second death.

What could be worse than one's soul being separated from our Creator for all eternity? The moment these souls realize the magnitude of their refusal to accept Jesus as Lord and Savior will be the single most terrifying moment in history—the moment that their names are not found in the Book of Life.

Remember, every knee will bow and every tongue will confess that Jesus Christ is Lord (Phil. 2:9–11).

Death and hades are now no more and will not plague the Lord's elect ever again, for the victory Jesus achieved on the cross is now fully realized as they join Satan, the beast, and the false prophet in the lake of fire for all eternity.

All that remains is the life and glory of the Lord.

Coming full circle, the perfect relationship between God and His creation, man, is now at hand—the relationship that has been designed since before the garden. These are really deep and impactful verses we read at the end of Revelation 20.

We are reading of the end of time. John writes that the current earth that we live on and the current heaven that God reigns in are done away with (v. 11). As Jesus enters into His complete reign as King of all, the sin-cursed heaven and earth cannot stand before His glory and perfection.

Which is kind of a strange concept to think about, isn't it? There was sin in heaven. We often think of it as a perfect place, but in its current form, the Bible contradicts this belief.

Now, am I saying that there is sin within God's heavenly courtroom before His throne? Not necessarily, but I'm not saying it does not exist. Remember, in the Book of Job (Job 1-2), Satan brought himself before God, who was on His throne.

So doesn't that imply heaven has been touched by the curse of sin, and this represents the need for both a new heaven and a new earth?

This is not to say that angels are going around sinning in heaven—or whatever souls have been granted access to it, if any. But heaven did experience sin within its reality because Satan sinned against God in his pride and was cast out of heaven.

Why don't we discuss this more as Christians? I cannot be the only one to find this a fascinating topic that has so much more depth held within the pages of the Bible.

Let's bring back group Bible studies, and not just for kids and youth groups but as a lifelong habit that grows and strengthens believers while diving deep into the rich Word of God!

At this moment when Jesus' supreme reign begins and the great white throne judgment commences, our world ends. All the continents; all the oceans; all the life crawling, swimming, and soaring across the face of the earth—gone.

It also begs the question: What is this going to look like on a cosmic scale?

With Satan's corruption of sin in the world God made, will the entire universe cease to be? Will it be some grand event, or will it simply cease to be in the span of a moment?

This is why I personally believe we as human beings will not succeed in colonizing another planet like Mars, which some, like Elon Musk, so desperately desire. I do not believe he wants this out of malice or to work against God; it is simply not something that will be allowed during this current era of creation.

"For God so loved the world" (John 3:16) means to me this one world that He created. Yes, He created every other heavenly body in existence, but only one has been proven to have intelligent, and designed, life on it.

Another out of the many questions that come to me for this time is: With a new heaven and a new earth will laws such as gravity, time, and reality exist as we know them?

Our time is based on the cycle of the sun and moon, both designed for the age of creation that will come to an end. And we will be given new, perfect bodies that will not know sin and death.

Will we have to eat, sleep, drink, and do all the other high-maintenance activities that these temporary bodies have to endure to survive? Will we ever tire on the new earth, or could we just go on an adventure of exploration that lasts as long as we care for it to?

With so many questions on the tongues of those who know and are secure in their belief that their names are written in the Lamb's Book of Life, we can all take solace in the fact that this end of the world is indeed coming, but it is a joyous event for those who have accepted salvation given by grace through faith in Jesus Christ.

For those who have not it is the worst day in the history of creation. They are past the point of redemption and repentance. They rejected the gift of salvation—that Jesus bridged the way for us through the shedding of His innocent and powerful blood on the cross and His triumphant victory over sin, death, and hades when He resurrected back to life on the third day, the day of victory.

They now share the same horrific fate as Lucifer, the angel who allowed pride (there's that word again) to set into motion not only his own demise but the demise of billions whom he managed to deceive into thinking they knew better than God.

CHAPTER 21

A NEW HEAVEN, EARTH, and JERUSALEM

I CAN ONLY SPEAK for myself, but I am very jealous that John gets to witness perhaps the most awe-inspiring event outside of creation itself: the future era of eternity, free of sin.

John stands on and recognizes (in a humble way) his apostolic authority by identifying himself yet again, of sound mind and spirit, as the witness to the Lord's new reality after sin and death have been defeated permanently (Rev. 21:2).

A new creation, a new beginning. For sin and the memory of Satan had permeated the old creation, so they had to be done away with. A clean and pure world, the utopia that mankind aspires to build yet fails so miserably to in doing so, is now a reality for the kingdom of God.

But what a difference this new world will be! John tells us that there will be no sea in it (v. 1)! Can you imagine? The element that is necessary for life in this current world we live in is water. That's not to say there is no water there, but no large bodies of water like the oceans we know of today.

Will we have other attributes of this current world? Will we be on a spherical planetoid for this new earth? Will it be flat? How large will it be to accommodate its inhabitants and their new, righteous bodies?

We will get some answers to these questions a little further into the chapter.

This is where we are going to spend eternity! A place that will never know the corrupting touch of sin. Will we even have animals in the same spirit as they were in the Garden of Eden? I would like to think one day my little Scooby will be in heaven with me, but it is not a certainty, as mankind is made differently than animals (in the image of God and with His life breathed into us).

But there are much greater things going on than just wondering what the new earth will look like. God's crown jewel, His Holy City, New Jerusalem, will take its place as the capital city of the new earth: "I, John, saw the holy city, New Jerusalem, coming down out of heaven from God, prepared as a bride adorned for her husband. And I heard a loud voice from heaven saying, 'Behold, the tabernacle of God is with men, and He will dwell with them'" (vv. 2–3).

This magnificent event, the joining of God's tabernacle with His people, is the unifying event we've all been waiting for since the fall in the Garden of Eden. We will no longer be separated from our Creator. We will walk in communion with Him daily. No more tears. No more pain. No more fear. No more doubt.

No more separation between God and His creation, for mankind has been cleansed by the blood of the Lamb and found righteous. This has allowed the reunification with God the Father to take place.

Just living in the fruit of the Spirit every moment of our lives.

The life that we are so used to and are hung up on, this sin-cursed life that we fear leaving in death, is no more. It's almost hard to fathom such a drastic change in reality, but it is in the Bible and thus is the truth about what is to come.

We just have to accept it and not base the end of time on our own understanding, but on the understanding of God's Word, which literally spells out what is to come for us and the consequences of not aligning ourselves with His will, order, and design.

It all boils down to one question: Will we choose life (God's way) or death (Satan's or our way)?

This is so important to realize, and God Himself even spells it out for us, as John witnesses the Father sitting on the throne in His glory. As the spring of life flows from His presence, God lists those who will not be with Him in eternity (v. 8):

- the cowardly (taking no action, hiding, disobeying the commands of the Lord)
- the unbelieving (the unfaithful)
- the abominable (given to the works of flesh, breaking the commandments of God)
- the murderers (takers of innocent life, abortion)
- the sexually immoral (all sexual activity outside biblical marriage)
- the sorcerers (mediums, diviners, those who alter people's minds and perspectives, drug dealers)
- the idolaters (worshippers of anything other than God)
- the liars (Jesus is the truth, and they deny Him with their false words)

In fact, the words that God Himself speaks to John are so important, I'm going to put them right here:

> It is done! I am the Alpha and the Omega, the Beginning and the End. I will give of the fountain of the water of life freely to him who thirsts. He who overcomes shall inherit all things, and I will be his God and he shall be My son. But the cowardly, unbelieving, abominable, murderers, sexually immoral, sorcerers, idolaters, and all liars shall have their part in the lake which burns with fire and brimstone, which is the second death.
> —REVELATION 21:6–8

A New Heaven, Earth, and Jerusalem

Please, to anyone reading this, take God at His word! He freely gives us the opportunity to seize abundant life as His children! But we must work for it!

If we overcome, meaning if we run the good race as Paul did, Christianity is not a stagnant way of life but a constant, ever-moving one that does have moments of tranquility and rest. But we are literally in a fight for our lives and the lives of those we encounter.

John, after recognizing the angel from the previous events of the bowls judgment, is shown the bride of Christ, represented as the Holy City of Jerusalem. There is so much represented here—the importance of Jerusalem not only to the Jews but to God. Yet the nations continue to try to separate her from the Lord.

It also shows just how important and holy the Lord views the institution of marriage, for even Jesus has a pure bride.

The sacredness of the relationship has been corrupted beyond measure on the earth. Premarital sex runs rampant even within the church, and divorce is prevalent—again, even within the church. Men and women act on their fleshly desires in an affront to God instead of dying to their flesh and living a sanctified life, and now we are seeing people reject the very bodies they have been given by the Lord and mutilate them into something they were never made to be.

Just as the Lord designed the Holy City of Jerusalem, so too did He design His creation—with purpose, with order, with righteousness, and with morality.

If His ways are good and holy, then any direction the enemy tries to steer people, away from His design and order, is not in any way good, righteous, or beneficial to the people.

As we continue through chapter 21, we really see writings from John that (again) obliterate any and every argument for the replacement theology, where the Christian church has replaced the nation of Israel when it comes to prophecy and the heart of God.

John describes the Holy City of Jerusalem in great detail, and what is the recurring theme we see here? Twelve. Twelve gates; twelve angels; twelve tribes of the children of Israel; twelve foundations; twelve apostles (all of whom were of Jewish ethnicity); twelve thousand furlongs in measure; a 144-cubit wall (twelve by twelve); twelve precious stones in the foundation; and twelve pearls that make up the twelve gates (vv. 14–21).

Have you caught on to the pattern yet? Twelve. It is the number that, according to a variety of sources, represents the completeness of God's perfect government, or reign.

It should be noted that this is not based on numerology, which is an unbiblical practice that puts power behind the numbers, but it is instead representative of God's choice and decision to use certain numbers for certain endeavors, which often are repeated throughout biblical history.

The twelve tribes of Israel, the twelve disciples, the twelve gates of Jerusalem—the numbers in and of themselves hold no power but instead represent what God wants them to, for He is the One who holds all the power and glory.

Do the types of precious stones also ring a bell to you? If you've ever read the Old Testament in its entirety, they should. While not identical, they are very close to the stones used in the priests' garments, which are (Exod. 39:10–13):

- sardius (carnelian in the ESV)
- topaz
- emerald (carbuncle in the ESV)
- turquoise
- sapphire
- diamond
- jacinth (ligure in the KJV)

- agate
- amethyst
- beryl
- onyx
- jasper

Meanwhile, the twelve foundations of New Jerusalem are adorned with twelve precious stones as well (Rev. 21:19–20):

- jasper
- sapphire
- chalcedony (agate in the ESV)
- emerald
- onyx (ESV)
- sardius
- chrysolite
- beryl
- topaz
- chrysoprase
- jacinth
- amethyst

So there are some overlaps with jasper, sapphire, agate, emerald, onyx, beryl, and topaz, but it's not an exact replica of the gems used.

But each time, there are twelve stones used by the Lord.

Again, it's not the numbers; it's the Lord's decision to use those numbers to represent what He wants them to represent.

This new reality, this new world, will be unlike anything of this old world and will be beyond our imagination. There will be no more day or night! John tells us that God's glory, which no longer will be hidden from His creation but will reside in the Holy City with us, will be our light (v. 23).

So then, will these bodies no longer use energy the way we do now? Will there be no need for sleep, and instead we'll get to enjoy the glory of His magnificent presence for eternity? It does not seem right to say "all day, every day" anymore because the entire format of timekeeping will be null and void during eternity—especially if there is no more day and no more night.

There is just God now.

No sun, no moon—will there be constellations dotting the sky, or would it even be possible with all things being illuminated by the light of God and His holiness?

One thing is for certain: Even in this new world, we can expect to see the beauty of God's majesty the same way we see it when we look out over natural landscapes here on earth. We are witnessing God's handiwork when we stand atop a mountain and look over a vast expanse of creation. This sense of awe and wonder will not be gone; if anything, it will be magnified in the new heaven and new earth, and that is something to look forward to with great expectation.

There will be no more decay, no more aging, in both nature and ourselves because the era of eternity begins here, in the perfection and light of the Lamb.

CHAPTER 22

The FINAL WORDS of the LORD

THIS IS THE last chapter of the Bible—the final twenty-one verses detailing what is to come and urging readiness for the end.

John has now seen scenes that would have killed men in the Old Testament, standing before God and seeing Him face-to-face. John has done this, viewing the Lord in the Spirit sitting atop His throne from which the river of life now flows, and on its banks grows the tree of life whose fruit was available in the garden.

> And he showed me a pure river of water of life, clear as crystal, proceeding from the throne of God and of the Lamb....On either side of the river, was the tree of life, which bore twelve fruits.
> —REVELATION 22:1–2

It's wild to think how similar things are from when they were first written in Genesis to how things will be in the end, or should I say beginning, in the new reality we will be living in.

How incredible is it that the one element scientists look for on planets as a sign of possible life is water,[1] which will now flow freely to us from the Creator of all things.

Jesus confirms so much to John for us to read and store within our souls. His repeating three times that He is coming soon—and quickly, like a thief in the night—cannot be overlooked or downplayed in terms of how important these statements are for Christians to hear, understand, and adhere to (vv. 7, 12, 20).

When we see repetitions like this throughout the Bible, it

is because the message God is trying to get across to us—His people, the faithful—is of vital importance. Jesus' return is literally a life-and-death scenario for all humanity that so many do not take even remotely seriously or even believe in.

He is coming, and He is taking with Him to the Holy City, Jerusalem, those who laid down their lives for Him and obeyed His commandments. Jesus also confirms here, again, His oneness with the Father (vv. 13–14). By His willful submission on the cross, death and sin were overcome, and in this new world we will live in, the curse of sin will be no more.

We as Christians are called to live by this very same willful submission that Christ demonstrated for us before the Father and to imitate this in our lives.

There has never been, nor will there ever be, hypocrisy on the part of Jesus when it comes to asking us to abide by His commandments, because He has already followed through on submitting to the Father's will and kept His commandments perfectly. Jesus is not asking us to do anything He has not already done Himself.

In fact, the words of Jesus in this final chapter of the most important book ever written are themselves so important because they hold within them the way to eternal life. Let's just go ahead and read over them now so that we can see why it is so important that Jesus Himself spoke them to John and put them in as some of the final words of the Bible.

- "Behold, I am coming quickly! Blessed is he who keeps the words of the prophecy of this book" (v. 7).
- "And behold, I am coming quickly, and My reward is with Me, to give to every one according to his work" (v. 12).
- "I am the Alpha and the Omega, the Beginning and the End, the First and the Last" (v. 13).

- "I, Jesus, have sent My angel to testify to you these things in the churches. I am the Root and the Offspring of David, the Bright and Morning Star" (v. 16).
- "Surely I am coming quickly" (v. 20).

In today's world the phrase "it goes without saying" has lost a lot—and I mean a lot—of meaning because all too often it does have to be said, as people are just not accepting truth when they hear it.

The words of Jesus are so important for Christians—all people, really, but those who declare His name especially—to pay attention to and hold on to as tribulation and persecution in life find them.

In verse 7 we hear Jesus say that those who keep "the words of the prophecy of this book" will be blessed. Now, I believe He is specifically referencing Revelation, but some may believe He is referring to the Bible, which does not change the message at all. Why? Because the Book of Revelation is an integral part of the Bible, and so His message remains the same, making it a subject not worth arguing over in the slightest.

We will be blessed reading the Bible—yes, true, 100 percent. But as the Book of Revelation says in the opening verses, and here again at the very end of the prophetic vision, we will be blessed when we hold fast to the words within the Revelation John was given.

It is a choice for each and every one of us to make: opening up the Word of God and spending necessary time in it. Spiritual growth comes from reading the Word, obeying the commandments of the Word, spending time in prayer and relationship with the Father, and living a life of righteousness and obedience in accordance with His Word.

Can we also take note—and in turn hold fast to this word of warning in our hearts and in what we engage with in life—that we get a list, again, of those who will live outside the kingdom of God? And the only place that will exist after the great white throne judgment is hell.

Here is the rundown, according to the New King James Version (v. 15). (Please compare the wording to other translations; the message remains the same.)

- Dogs (This is not the first time the Bible uses this term to refer to Gentiles, or the immoral.)
- Sorcerers (This includes dealers of drugs that alter reality for people.)
- The sexually immoral (The Bible focuses so much on how sexual immorality grieves the Lord; this subject needs to be taught much more than it is.)
- Murderers (These are takers of innocent blood, such as abortionists.)
- Idolaters (This term refers to those who worship things other than the Lord. Where you spend your time is where your heart lies.)
- Lovers and practitioners of lies (If Jesus is the truth, anything contrary to what He teaches, along with the words of the Bible, is false.)

All we have to do is look around our country these days to see that our society, in general, has abandoned these principles of God and lives lifestyles that the Bible warns are ways to not get into heaven.

Go back and read the letters to the end-times churches. See how Jesus issues correction to those in need of it. This puts to rest the argument of "once saved, always saved," which has deceived many into living unholy and abominable lives.

I do not use words like these for shock factor or to show

off my vocabulary. Trust me, if you are reading this, you are probably smarter than I am. But there is power in words, and the Bible specifically uses these terms to convey how God truly feels when people commit such heinous acts against His sovereignty.

He hates sin. He cannot stand it, and He will most definitely not, *not*, allow people given to such lifestyles into His new and perfect kingdom.

Are we going to live sin-free and perfect lives as Christians? No, quite the opposite. But are we going to strive for holiness, to consecrate our lives and give up the things that make us stumble, and to work day after day to draw close to the Lord?

It is what's in our hearts, which will dictate our actions, that matters the most. We will stumble, even fall, at times. But are we going to pick ourselves up, dust ourselves off, and continue on the straight and narrow path?

I pray that we all do, for the alternative is eternity separated from our Lord.

> For I testify to everyone who hears the words of the prophecy of this book: If anyone adds to these things, God will add to him the plagues that are written in this book; and if anyone takes away from the words...God shall take away his part from the Book of Life.
> —REVELATION 22:18–19

How important is the warning that John the revelator—and more than that, the inspired Word of God—gives (and which Jesus also warns of during His final words in Revelation) that no man-made changes, additions, or retractions occur to God's Word? Man is sinful and fallible, unable to weave the perfection and righteousness of God's redemption story for His creation.

Today, many who claim to believe in the Lord are actively

contradicting the words held within the Bible with their actions, rhetoric, and tolerance for things that the Lord finds detestable.

There is only one way to live a victorious life and receive the gift of eternal life: to read, meditate on, and obey the words found within the pages of the Holy Bible. By doing this we come to the realization that Jesus Christ is the Messiah, the Savior for all humanity, and that God has a plan of redemption for us all.

It is up to us to receive this gift, bought with the precious and powerful blood of Jesus. There is still much work to do, and prophetic events have yet to take place before the judgment of the sin-cursed earth, but we are well on our way there. We are living in accelerated times, and Jesus warns in this very chapter that He is coming, and coming soon. We must live in expectation of His arrival, or we will be caught unawares, like the five foolish virgins, and miss the wedding of the Bridegroom.

I can only speak for myself when I say this is the single most important decision we can make in life: to accept the truth of who Jesus is and what He came to earth to do.

CONCLUSION

Well, if you have made it this far in the book, I can only say thank you.

The Book of Revelation is so important to Christians for a variety of reasons. God must think so as well because He had John tell us that we would be blessed just by reading it!

Every single book of the holy Scriptures is important; that's why they are grouped together to create the canonical Bible. However, certain books hold different places in our hearts.

For me Revelation has always been my favorite book of the Bible. I love reading the visions John was given regarding the end of the world, as well as Satan's ultimate defeat. But as I've grown older, as I've matured physically and spiritually, this book has more relevance in our world today than I feel it ever has.

We are clearly on a collision course with the end-times, and the way things are heading, there are many passages in the Revelation that John was given that are turning out to be literal interpretations (in my belief—I find the evidence within our world to be irrefutable, from an honest perspective).

I believe this is in part due to the commands Jesus gives us, not just in Revelation but in the Gospels as well. We are to pay attention to both the good and the bad events taking place around the world and within the church.

As Christians we shout for joy along with heaven as each new soul accepts Jesus as their Lord and Savior, and we pray for the repentance of our nation, which in turn will see another Great Awakening shake the souls of citizens across the land. We yearn for these powerful moves of God as we make Him the top priority and repent of our sinful, prideful ways that have shifted our focus away from the Lord.

Yet at the same time, we must be aware that things are going to get worse before the return of Jesus Christ. We are called to the front lines of spiritual warfare against the enemy and to be participants in our society, not hiding in the shadows or merely standing on the sidelines while the world careens off course even further away from God and His original design for it.

Apostasy just does not feel like it is a word that gets used much these days, and when it does, it is quickly dismissed. It is not a word meant to bring judgment, but awareness and repentance.

There is a wave of apostate churches appearing in the West—churches that have abandoned the ways of God as described in His written Word. Entire denominations have abandoned the ways of God's Word and embraced the ways of the world.

Revelation teaches us how to course correct with the letters to the end-times churches, but for us to have any effect in showing those who have turned their backs on God the error of their ways, there must be love in our hearts.

We see clearly the fate awaiting the apostate church, which wraps the Bible with their ideologies instead of wrapping their worldviews with the Bible.

The greatest thing we as Christians can do for this world is to take Jesus—whom we confess as our Lord and Savior, as well as the ultimate example of how to live our lives—at His word. By doing so, we will obey His commands and live our lives with a sense of urgency, engaging in ministry and outreach to a world that desperately needs a relationship with its Creator.

If we don't do it, then who will? If the lost do not have a radical encounter with Jesus because we did not do what we were called to do, we will answer for it on the day that our deeds are read before the great white throne judgment. Is that something any of us want to answer to Jesus for? That because of our indifference and inaction, we failed in our commission?

Jesus says to be ready, for He is coming soon and quickly. While there are prophecies from other parts of the Bible still to be fulfilled, no one knows the day or time of His return or how quickly the events that must take place for Jesus' return will actually happen.

It is imperative for each and every one of us to be ready, to be sanctified, and to be busy carrying out the works of Jesus, as we are commanded to do as Christians.

I leave you with a section of Scripture that calls us to action and is not found in the Book of Revelation, but instead is from the book of my namesake, James:

> Therefore lay aside all filthiness and overflow of wickedness, and receive with meekness the implanted word, which is able to save your souls.
>
> But be doers of the word, and not hearers only, deceiving yourselves. For if anyone is a hearer of the word and not a doer, he is like a man observing his natural face in a mirror; for he observes himself, goes away, and immediately forgets what kind of man he was. But he who looks into the perfect law of liberty and continues in it, and is not a forgetful hearer but a doer of the work, this one will be blessed in what he does.
>
> If anyone among you thinks he is religious, and does not bridle his tongue but deceives his own heart, this one's religion is useless. Pure and undefiled religion before God and the Father is this: to visit orphans and widows in their trouble, and to keep oneself unspotted from the world.
>
> —JAMES 1:21–27

I cannot explain it any better than the Word of God does, nor do I have the wisdom or authority behind the words.

So please, heed the Word of God, and let us all consecrate ourselves before the Lord, performing ministry in His name in service of Him. And let's not kid ourselves and live self-delusional lives, thinking we are something we are not when we ignore His commands and live lives focused on our own wants and desires.

Because just like the Revelation and the Bible as a whole, our lives are to be all about Him.

A PERSONAL INVITATION to KNOW JESUS

GOD LOVES YOU deeply. His Word is filled with promises that reveal His desire to bring healing, hope, and abundant life to every area of your being—body, mind, and spirit. More than anything, He wants a personal relationship with you through His Son, Jesus Christ.

If you've never invited Jesus into your life, you can do so right now. It's not about religion—it's about a relationship with the One who knows you completely and loves you unconditionally. If you're ready to take that step, simply pray this prayer with a sincere heart:

> *Lord Jesus, I want to know You as my Savior and Lord. I confess and believe that You are the Son of God and that You died for my sins. I believe You rose from the dead and are alive today. Please forgive me for my sins. I invite You into my heart and my life. Make me new. Help me to walk with You, grow in Your love, and live for You every day. In Jesus' name, amen.*

If you just prayed that prayer, you've made the most important decision of your life. All heaven rejoices with you, and so do I! You are now a child of God, and your journey with Him has just begun. Please contact my publisher at pray4me@charismamedia.com so that we can send you some materials that will help you become established in your relationship with the Lord. We look forward to hearing from you.

NOTES

CHAPTER 1

1. Christian Pure Team, "The Fates of the Disciples: How Each of Jesus' Apostles Met Their End," Christian Pure, accessed April 14, 2025, https://christianpure.com/learn/disciples-fates-jesus-apostles-deaths/; Tommi Waters, "Matthew the Apostle: Story, Facts, and Death," Study.com, updated November 21, 2023, https://study.com/academy/lesson/matthew-the-apostle-history-facts-death.html; "How Did Apostle John Die?," Bible Hub, accessed April 14, 2025, https://biblehub.com/q/how_did_apostle_john_die.htm; *Encyclopedia Britannica*, "St. Simon the Apostle," accessed April 14, 2025, https://www.britannica.com/biography/Saint-Simon-the-Apostle; "St. Jude Thaddeus Symbols," The National Shrine of St. Jude, accessed April 14, 2025, https://shrineofstjude.org/the-shrine/st-jude/st-jude-thaddeus-symbols/.
2. *New Catholic Encyclopedia*, "Asia, Roman Province of," Encyclopedia.com, accessed April 14, 2025, https://www.encyclopedia.com/religion/encyclopedias-almanacs-transcripts-and-maps/asia-roman-province.
3. Blue Letter Bible, "*martys*," accessed April 14, 2025, https://www.blueletterbible.org/lexicon/g3144/kjv/tr/0-1.
4. Clyde E. Fant and Mitchell G. Reddish, "Patmos," in *A Guide to Biblical Sites in Greece and Turkey* (Oxford Academic, 2003), 92–100.
5. Jack W. Hayford, ed., *New Spirit-Filled Life Bible* (Thomas Nelson Inc., 2002), 1, 818.

CHAPTER 2

1. "Who Were the Nicolaitans and What Was Their Doctrine and Deeds?" Renner Ministries, accessed April 16, 2025, https://renner.org/article/who-were-the-nicolaitans-and-what-was-their-doctrine-and-deeds.
2. Janene Keeth, "Smyrna: The Suffering Church," Bible.org, January 25, 2008, https://bible.org/seriespage/3-smyrna-suffering-church.

3. Janene Keeth, "Pergamum: The Compromising Church," Bible.org, January 25, 2008, https://bible.org/seriespage/4-pergamum-compromising-church.
4. Elena Chabo, "Welcome to Beauty Witchcraft's Modern Resurgence," *Cosmopolitan*, updated June 18, 2024, https://www.cosmopolitan.com/uk/beauty-hair/a60658740/beauty-witchcraft-glamour-magick; Amanda Arnold, "The First Ladies Who Brought the Occult to the White House," *Vice*, July 12, 2017, https://www.vice.com/en/article/the-first-ladies-who-brought-witchcraft-to-the-white-house/; "Six Movies that Weave Real Witchcraft into Their Narratives," Magick and Witchcraft, accessed April 16, 2025, https://www.magickandwitchcraft.com/post/witchcraft-movies; Catarina Elvira, "The Evolution of Occultism in Gaming," Atmostfear Entertainment, accessed April 16, 2025, https://www.atmostfear-entertainment.com/medias/games/evolution-occultism-gaming/.
5. Antonio Pagliarulo, "Why Paganism and Witchcraft Are Making a Comeback," NBC News, October 30, 2022, https://www.nbcnews.com/think/opinion/paganism-witchcraft-are-making-comeback-rcna54444.
6. Karen Hardin and Jessilyn Lancaster, "America Just Erected a Gateway to Demonic Darkness," *Charisma News*, October 4, 2018, https://charismanews.com/opinion/america-just-erected-a-gateway-to-demonic-darkness.
7. James Lasher, "Pagan Statue Erected on New York City Courthouse," *Charisma News*, January 26, 2023, https://charismanews.com/news/us/pagan-statue-erected-on-new-york-courthouse.

Chapter 3

1. Ed Stetzer, "Pentecostals: How Do They Keep Growing While Other Groups Are Declining?," *Church Leaders*, June 27, 2023, https://churchleaders.com/voices/453879-pentecostals-how-do-they-keep-growing.html.
2. Sean Nelson, "Why Nigeria Is the Most Dangerous Country in the World for Christians," ADF

International, June 18, 2024, https://adfinternational.org/commentary/nigeria-most-dangerous-country-christians.
3. Jon Brown, "Embattled Canadian Pastor Who Faced Jail Time for Sermon Appeals 'Outrageous' Guilty Verdict," *The Christian Post*, October 19, 2023, https://www.christianpost.com/news/embattled-canadian-pastor-artur-pawlowski-appeals-guilty-verdict.html.
4. James Lasher and Charisma Media Staff, "The Mystery of Apostasy with Jonathan Cahn," *Charisma*, May 15, 2023, https://mycharisma.com/propheticrevival/propheticinsight/the-mystery-of-apostasy-with-jonathan-cahn.

Chapter 5

1. Lewis E. Jones, "Would You Be Free from the Burden of Sin?," Hymnary.org, accessed April 21, 2025, https://hymnary.org/text/would_you_be_free_from_the_burden_jones.

Chapter 6

1. Bidur Adhikari, "Human Rights Is Just a Story—[Yuval Noah] Harari," YouTube, January 23, 2024, https://www.youtube.com/watch?v=MjWJb3dzsc8.
2. Melissa Pistilli, "How Would a New BRICS Currency Affect the US Dollar?," Nasdaq.com, March 18, 2025, https://www.nasdaq.com/articles/how-would-new-brics-currency-affect-us-dollar-updated-2024.
3. "Ben Shapiro Says Multiculturalism May Bring About 'Downfall of Western Civilization' in Latest 'Facts' Episode," *The Daily Wire*, November 8, 2023, https://www.dailywire.com/news/ben-shapiro-says-multiculturalism-may-bring-about-downfall-of-western-civilization-in-latest-facts-episode.
4. "World Population by Country in 2025," Database.Earth, accessed April 21, 2025, https://database.earth/population/by-country/2025.

Chapter 7

1. Greg Denham, "A Christian's Relationship and Responsibility to Israel," *All Israel News*, February 18, 2024, https://allisrael.com/blog/a-christian-s-relationship-and-responsibility-to-israel.
2. Blue Letter Bible, "*angelos*," accessed April 22, 2025, https://www.blueletterbible.org/lexicon/g32/kjv/tr/0-1.

Chapter 8

1. *Encyclopedia Britannica*, "Indian Ocean Tsunami of 2004," accessed April 23, 2025, https://www.britannica.com/event/Indian-Ocean-tsunami-of-2004.
2. "The Yangtze: Asia's Longest River," World Wide Fund for Nature UK, accessed April 23, 2025, https://www.wwf.org.uk/where-we-work/places/yangtze-asias-longest-river.

Chapter 9

1. Warhammer 40,000 Wiki, "Abaddon," accessed April 23, 2025, https://warhammer40k.fandom.com/wiki/Abaddon.
2. *Encyclopedia Britannica*, "sulfur," accessed April 23, 2025, https://www.britannica.com/science/sulfur; "Sulfur," Minerals Education Coalition, accessed April 23, 2025, https://mineralseducationcoalition.org/minerals-database/sulfur/.
3. Ronn Blitzer, "California Bill to Lower Penalties for Sexual Relations with Minor Heads to Newsom's Desk," Fox News, September 3, 2020, https://www.foxnews.com/politics/california-bill-lower-penalties-sexual-relations-with-minor-newsom.

Chapter 10

1. "The Basilica of St. John in Ephesus," Ertunga Ecir, accessed April 23, 2025, https://ertungaecir.com/blog/the-basilica-of-st-john-in-ephesus/.
2. Bryan Windle, "Evidence from Ephesus for the Reliability of Scripture," Bible Archaeology Report,

accessed April 23, 2025, https://biblearchaeologyreport.com/2017/11/06/evidence-from-ephesus-for-the-reliability-of-scripture/.
3. Cris Coleman, "Did John Ever Taste of Death?," The Biblical Apologist, April 16, 2011, https://biblicalapologist.blogspot.com/2011/04/did-john-ever-taste-of-death.html.

CHAPTER 11

1. "Frequently Asked Questions," Temple Institute, accessed April 24, 2025, https://templeinstitute.org/frequently-asked-questions.
2. "The Mystery of the Red Heifer: Divine Promise of Purity," Temple Institute, accessed April 24, 2025, https://templeinstitute.org/red-heifer.

CHAPTER 12

1. Hayford, *New Spirit-Filled Life Bible*, 1, 832.
2. Tim Pearce, "Majority of Students at Top-Ranking Universities Say Anti-Semitism a Problem on Campus," *The Daily Wire*, May 13, 2024, https://www.dailywire.com/news/majority-of-students-at-top-ranking-universities-say-anti-semitism-a-problem-on-campus.
3. Michael Brown, "The Ominous Resurfacing of 'Christian' Antisemitism," *The Christian Post*, July 20, 2024, https://www.christianpost.com/voices/the-ominous-resurfacing-of-christian-antisemitism.html.

CHAPTER 13

1. Oxford Reference, "blasphemy," accessed April 25, 2025, https://www.oxfordreference.com/display/10.1093/oi/authority.20110803095511445.
2. "Man Accused of Destroying Satanic Temple Display at Iowa Capitol Is Now Charged with Hate Crime," Associated Press, accessed April 25, 2025, https://apnews.com/article/satanic-temple-hate-crime-iowa-cb182f8b3235d25fd4949e0b2e4f43f7.
3. Simon Constable, "Klaus Schwab's World Economic Forum in Davos Exposed as Place Where 'Cronyism

Can Flourish,'" *Fox News*, January 21, 2024, https://www.foxnews.com/world/klaus-schwabs-world-economic-forum-davos-exposed-place-cronyism-can-flourish.
4. "Nigeria," Open Doors USA, accessed April 25, 2025, https://www.opendoors.org/en-US/persecution/countries/nigeria.
5. Steve Warren, "Canadian Pastor Acquitted After Pandemic Police Hunted Him and His Church with a Helicopter," *CBN News*, November 2, 2022, https://www2.cbn.com/news/world/canadian-pastor-acquitted-after-pandemic-police-hunted-him-and-his-church-helicopter.
6. Mary Margaret Olohan, "Republicans to Hold Hearing on DOJ Targeting Pro-Lifers," House Judiciary Committee Republicans, May 12, 2023, https://judiciary.house.gov/media/in-the-news/republicans-hold-hearing-doj-targeting-pro-lifers.
7. Brian Bushard, "Whole Foods Allows Customers to Pay with Palm Scanners—Here's How It Works," *Forbes*, July 20, 2023, https://www.forbes.com/sites/brianbushard/2023/07/20/whole-foods-allows-customers-to-pay-with-palm-scanners-heres-how-it-works.
8. Alex Mitchell et al., "Everything You Need to Know as Whole Foods' Palm Print Payments Take NYC—and Is It Safe?," *New York Post*, February 5, 2024, https://nypost.com/2024/02/05/tech/everything-to-know-as-whole-foods-palm-print-payments-take-nyc.
9. "About Facial Data," Amazon, accessed April 25, 2025, https://developer-docs.amazon.com/sp-api/docs/facial-data-privacy-policy.
10. Mitchell et al., "Everything You Need to Know."
11. Lillian Gissen, "Woman Who Married a 'Tech Genius' Reveals Her Husband Implanted a Chip in Her Hand—Which Serves as a Key to Their Mansion," *Daily Mail*, updated September 30, 2022, https://www.dailymail.co.uk/femail/article-11260109/Woman-reveals-tech-genius-husband-CHIP-serves-key-credit-card.html.

12. "Online Grocery Shopping in the United States—Statistics and Facts," Statista, accessed April 25, 2025, https://www.statista.com/topics/1915/online-grocery-shopping-in-the-united-states/#topicOverview.
13. Alex Bitter and Dominic Reuter, "Locked-Up Merchandise at Drugstores Is Annoying Shoppers—and It's Getting Worse," *Business Insider*, August 8, 2024, https://www.businessinsider.com/locked-up-merchandise-drugstores-annoys-shoppers-cvs-walgreens-rite-aid-2024-8.

Chapter 14

1. Kat Teurfs et al., "What Did Lori Vallow Daybell Do? A Full Timeline of the 'Doomsday Mom' Case," CBS News, accessed April 25, 2025, https://www.cbsnews.com/news/lori-vallow-chad-daybell-what-did-they-do-doomsday-mom-murders-case-timeline.
2. Meredith Deliso, "'Doomsday Mom' Lori Daybell Delivers Opening Statement in Her Latest Murder Trial," ABC News, April 7, 2025, https://abcnews.go.com/US/lori-daybell-arizona-murder-trial-opening-statements/story?id=120499584.

Chapter 16

1. Blue Letter Bible, *"mikros,"* accessed April 27, 2025, https://www.blueletterbible.org/lexicon/g3398/kjv/tr/0-1/; Blue Letter Bible, *"megas,"* accessed April 27, 2025, https://www.blueletterbible.org/lexicon/g3173/kjv/tr/0-1/.
2. Jordan B. Peterson, host, Jordan B. Peterson Podcast, "Detransition: The Wounds that Won't Heal—Chloe Cole," *The Daily Wire*, January 2, 2023, 2 hr., 5 mins., https://www.dailywire.com/podcasts/the-jordan-b-peterson-podcast/transition-of-minors-is-malpractice-chloe-cole.
3. Paolo D'Odorico et al., "The Global Value of Water in Agriculture," *Proceedings of the National Academy of Sciences of the United States of America* 117, no. 36 (2020): 21985–21993, https://www.pnas.org/doi/

full/10.1073/pnas.2005835117; "Why Is Water So Important for Life as We Know It?," Astrobiology at NASA, accessed April 27, 2025, https://astrobiology.nasa.gov/education/alp/water-so-important-for-life/.
4. Michael Hollan, "How to Talk to Hoarders About Stockpiling Items," Fox News, April 26, 2020, https://www.foxnews.com/lifestyle/how-to-talk-to-people-about-stockpiling-items.

Chapter 18

1. ACLU, "Overturning Roe Is Just the Beginning," American Civil Liberties Union, June 24, 2024, https://www.aclu.org/news/reproductive-freedom/overturning-roe-is-just-the-beginning.

Chapter 20

1. Stephen Strang, "How Cancel Culture Has Impacted the Church, America, and You," *Charisma News*, January 27, 2022, https://charismanews.com/culture/how-cancel-culture-has-impacted-the-church-america-and-you.

Chapter 22

1. Andrew Greenspan, "Water Beyond Earth: The Search for the Life-Sustaining Liquid," Science in the News, accessed August 17, 2024, https://sitn.hms.harvard.edu/flash/2019/water-beyond-earth-the-search-for-the-life-sustaining-liquid.

ACKNOWLEDGMENTS

Writing this book has been quite the journey, and I could never have completed it alone. There are so many people I want to thank, and while I can't list everyone, know that I appreciate each of you more than I can say.

First, to my wife, Victoria—you never stopped believing in me, even when I wasn't sure this book would ever see the light of day. Your encouragement kept me going, and I am beyond grateful for your unwavering support.

To my mother, Phyllis—you never stopped praying, not just for me but for our entire family and for this book. Your prayers carried me through; I know they made a difference in completing this project.

To Robert Caggiano—thank you for giving me that push when I needed it most. Your encouragement and help in getting the submission and proposal process started played a huge role in making this book a reality.

To everyone involved in the editing, marketing, and production process—this book would not exist without you. Thank you for your hard work, dedication, and expertise in bringing it all together.

Finally, to my heavenly Father—this book began as a dream You placed on my heart while I was away from my family, spending my weeks alone in hotel rooms. But I was never truly alone. You were right there with me, guiding me, giving me insight, and reminding me of the purpose behind every word. Thank You for walking with me through this journey and for making this book possible.

To everyone who picks up this book and reads it—thank you. My prayer is that it blesses and encourages you as much as the process of writing it has shaped me.